# Primary History

# Kingdom of Benin

# The complete volume

*Fidelia Nimmons*

# Contents

| | |
|---|---|
| Kingdom of Benin :1 | 3 |
| Growing up in Benin : 2 | 60 |
| Historical enquiry: 3 | 111 |

# Inside A Rainforest Royal Court

## Kingdom of Benin: 1

*Fidelia Nimmons*

Contributors:

Hon Barrister Patrick Aigbogun
Bernadette Aigbogun
Chief Sunday Aigbogun (Late) Chief Ebenzer of Igueben

Text ©Fidelia Nimmons 2013

Fidelia Nimmons asserts the moral right to be identified as the author of this work.

All rights reserved. No part of this publication may be reproduced, stored in a retrieval system, or transmitted in any form or by any other means, electronic, mechanical, photocopying, recording or otherwise, without prior written permission from the author or in accordance with provision of the Copyright, Design and Patents Act 1988, or under the terms of any licence permitting copying issued by the Copyright Licensing Agency, 90 Tottenham Court Road, London W1P 9HE.

Preface

Great Kingdom of Benin, one of the greatest Kingdoms to exist in Africa, was at its height between the 14th and 16th century. Things changed with European colonisation of Africa in the 19th century. Its story however continues to intrigue and excite scholars and historians alike.

The kingdom's people hold fast to their ancestral customs, adapting when they need to e.g. in embracing Christianity and modern influences from other countries and cultures particularly the West.

How to use:
You will find a glossary at the end of the book which explains specialist words written in red throughout the book.

Words in the glossary are grouped according to the section where they are used.

Some brain teaser questions have been included at the back for those interested in a bit of challenge.

A list of websites for further reading is included at the back of the book under bibliography.

Volume 2 of this book: *Inside A Rainforest Court: Growing up* presents information on aspects of life for ordinary people such as Childhood and marriage.

Volume 3 of this book Kingdom of Benin: Historical enquiry provides scholars with numerous historical enquiry activities.

This book provides complete teaching and learning material into the study of Kingdom of Benin and African history and is suitable for scholars from key Stage 2 to GCE level.

# Contents

| | |
|---|---|
| Location | 7 |
| Background information | 8 |
| History timelines | 9 |
| A Bini Creation story | 11 |
| Government | 12 |
| Death and Burial | 26 |
| Trade and Commerce | 33 |
| Religion | 35 |
| Art | 38 |
| The King's Festival | 41 |
| Slavery | 45 |
| Food | 46 |
| End of Old Kingdom | 48 |
| Modern Benin | 51 |
| Glossary | 54 |
| Brain teasers | 59 |

# Location

Below is location of Great Kingdom of Benin before colonisation in Africa.

The modern kingdom is located in modern day Nigeria in West Africa.

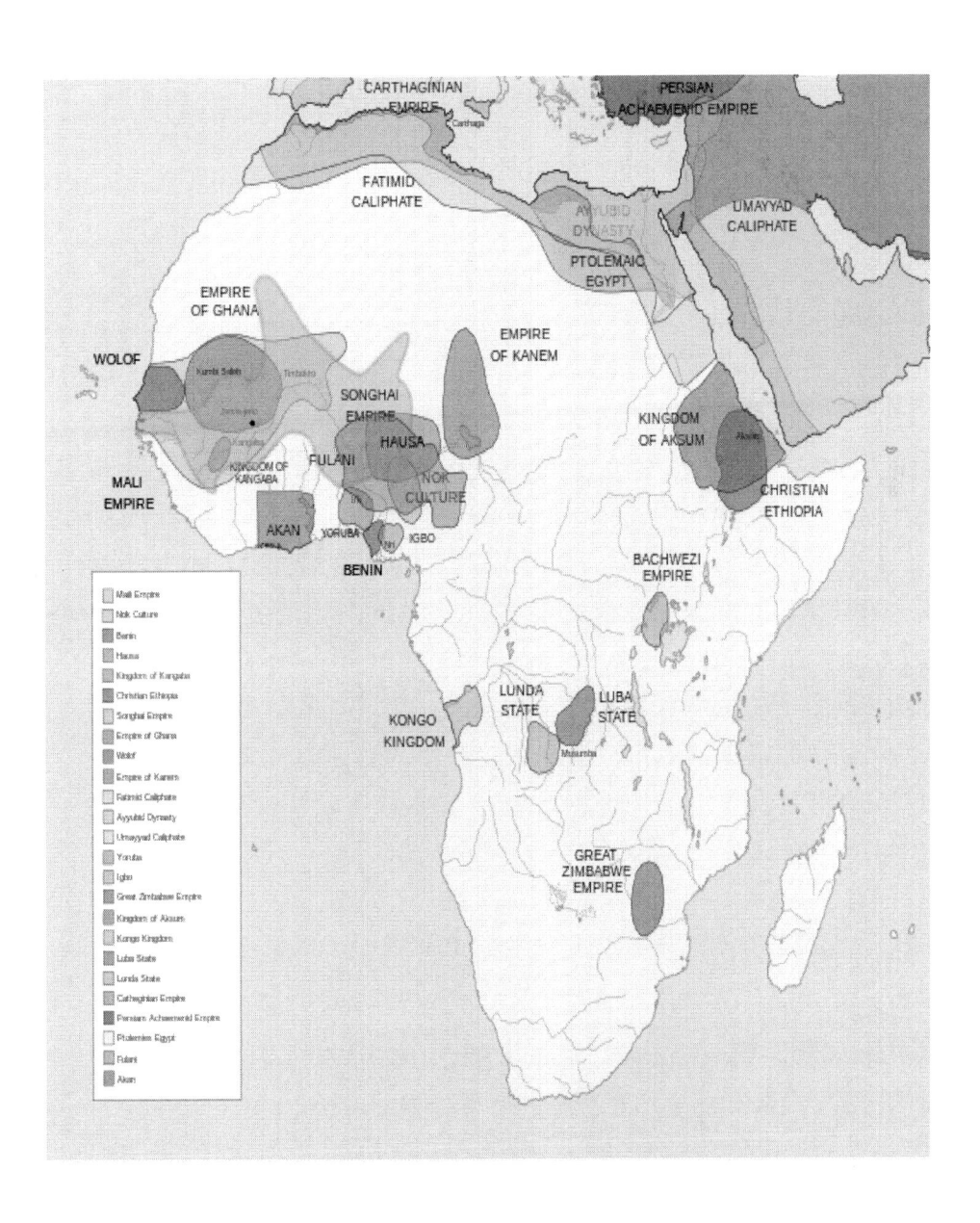

# Background information:

The Kingdom of Benin was one of the Forest Kingdoms of ancient Africa. It was founded by the Edo or Bini people during the 14th century, reached its height with a powerful Royal court in the 15th century, before it was finally conquered in the 19th century by the British.

The ancient Kingdom of Benin was located in present day Southern Nigeria, a country which did not exist at the time of its reign and which was formed during the scramble for Africa period, when European powers as a result of the Berlin conference of 1884 - 1885, carved and marked out artificial boundaries on African soil as their territories. The Kingdom of Benin kings resisted this change and this resistance eventually led to the kingdom's sacking during the Benin Punitive Expedition of 1897. This the British claimed was in response to massacre of their officials who had been obliterated by Benin soldiers for violating their custom of no foreign visitors during their king's ancestral festival. Britain's real reasons were expansion of its African territory and trade into the interiors of Africa which the king of Benin had stopped.

The Kingdom of Benin culture has not changed much since ancient times and traditions such as their royal family, chieftaincy, art, and oral folklore continue to thrive to this day as a way of preserving their customs and passing on their history to the next generation.

# History timelines

## World History Timeline

2686 - 525 BC
Ancient Egypt

40BC
Ubini (Benin) Kingdom founded

750 - 30 BC
Ancient Greece

146 BC - 400 AD
Ancient Rome

410 - 1065
Invaders

900 - 1100
Ogiso Kings rule Benin

1200
Oba Eweka begins
The Oba era in Benin

1216 - 1347
Middle Ages

1485 - 1602
Tudors

1819 - 1901
Victorians

1897
End of Ancient Benin

1914
Modern Benin

# Kings of Benin timeline

| | |
|---|---|
| EARLY PERIOD | Ogiso kings |
| | Oranmiyan |
| Early 14th century | 1. Eweka 1 |
| or before | 2. Uwakhuahen |
| | 3. Ehenmihen |
| | 4. Ewedo |
| c. late 14th century | 5. Oguola |
| | 6. Edoni |
| | 7. Udagbedo |
| c. early 15th century | 8. Ohen |
| | 9. Egbeka |
| | 10. Orobiru |
| | 11. Uwaifiokun |
| WARRIOR KINGS | 12. Ewuare |
| c. mid- 15th century | 13. Ezoti |
| | 14. Olua |
| c. late 15th century | 15. Ozolua |
| to early 16th century | 16. Esigie |
| | 17. Orhoghua |
| Late 16th century | 18. Ehengbuda |
| CRISIS AND RENEWAL | 19. Ohuan |
| | 20. Ohenzae |
| | 21. Akenzae |
| | 22. Akengboi |
| | 23. Akenkpaye |
| | 24. Akengbedo |
| | 25. Ore-oghenen |
| c. late 17th century | 26. Ewuakpe |
| | 27. Ozuere |
| c. 1715 | 28 Akenzua |
| c. 1735 | 29. Eresoyen |
| c.1750 | 30. Akengbuda |
| c.1804 | 31. Obanosa |
| | 32. Ogbebo |
| c.1815 | 33. Osemwede |
| c. 1850 | 34. Adolo |
| END OF THE KINGDOM | 35. Ovoranmwen |
| NEW PERIOD | 36. Eweka 11 |
| 1933 | 37. Akenzua 11 |
| 1979 | 38. Erediauwa |

# A Bini creation story.

In the beginning, there were no land, only waters.

At the centre of the waters stood a tree and on its top lived Owonwon, the toucan.

When Osanobua decided to populate the world, he gathered his three sons and sent them off in a canoe. Each was given the choice of one gift to take with him.

The two elder sons chose wealth and craft tools. As the youngest prepared to choose his own gift, Owonwon cried out to him to take a snail shell. This he did, and when the canoe reached the centre of the waters the youngest son turned the shell upside down and out poured an endless stream of sand. In this manner, the land began to emerge from the waters. The sons of Osanobua were afraid to go out of the canoe and so the chameleon was sent to test the firmness of the ground. From that time on, it walks with a hesitating step.

The place where the land emerged was called Agbon, "the world", at Agbon, Osanobua first came down from the sky on a chain and demarcated the world. It was from there that he sent people to the four corners of the earth, to every country and geographic realm. He made his youngest son the ruler of Benin, the owner of the land and he established his own realm, the spirit world, across the waters where the sky and earth meet.

So began the story of a kingdom that was to become great in time, a kingdom where the gods intermingled with people and their affairs on a daily basis; a kingdom where the people had to keep the gods happy to keep them on side; a kingdom whose king was a son of the chief god Osanobua; a king who had intimate relationships with the gods; a king with powers to intervene in the gods' decisions regarding the people and most important of all, a king who could switch easily between the tangible world and the spiritual realm.

# Government
# The Oba

**The Oba - *the divine kingship*. The Edo** believed that the Oba was divine, this was reflected in their day to day way of life and extended to all areas including political, religious and social aspects. Bini oral traditions, has it that the Oba descended from Oranmiyan, a Yoruba Prince from Ife whom they had invited to be their king when they became dissatisfied with their previous one. The Oba ruled on the virtue of this alone.

The Oba's political powers were extensive, he was the last resort in court matters and he alone could issue the death penalty. He owned all the land in the kingdom and all taxes and tributes were paid to him. He also controlled external trade. His army was well trained and the best during that time.

Benin Bronzes showing a Portuguese soldier with musket. The Portuguese trained the Benin army and fought alongside them in many wars.

# Court life

The Oba lived in a vast area of land to accommodate, residential areas for his numerous wives and small children, meeting chambers for various groups of chiefs, storehouses, shrines and alters and work areas for ritual specialists and royal craftsmen. In short the palace was a busy place; with hustling and bustling noises of activities carried out by the multitudes of officials, servants, family members and chiefs.

Early Dutch travellers described the royal palace as divided into many magnificent palaces, houses and apartments, and comprises beautiful and long square galleries, about as long as the Exchange at Amsterdam. The palace was said to be as large as the town of Haarlem.

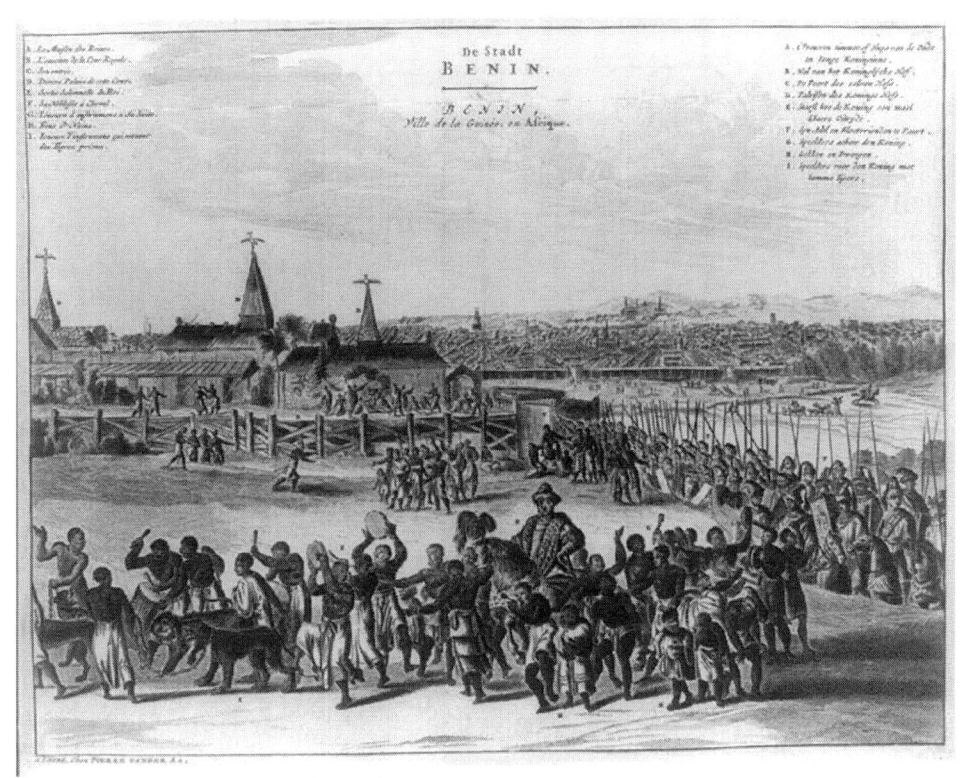

View of Benin City with Oba in procession engraved in early 17th century by Olfert Dapper (1668).

He described 'The Oba shews himself only once a year to his people, going out of his court on horseback, beautifully attired with all sorts of royal ornaments, and accompanied by three to four hundred noblemen on horseback and on foot, and a great number of musicians before and behind him, playing merry tunes on all sorts of instruments'.

The Oba on horse back

In Edo custom, only the Oba was allowed to ride side-saddle on his horse.
Here two attendants use their shields to shade him from the elements.

What jobs do you think the pages did in the palace?

# Administration

**The Ancient Chiefs**
The titled chiefs together with the royal family made up the political elites of the kingdom.

**Chieftaincy pecking order**
There three chiftancy groups with specialised dutietes. These were:

### 1) The Seven Uzama –
These were considered the descendants of the very elders of Benin who had sent to Ife for Oranmiyan.
They were the 'guardians of Benin custom'.
They installed new kings.
They took active roles in the annual worship of the departed ones.

### 2) The Palace Chiefs -
They lived in ogbe- the king's sector of the city.
They were members of well established urban families.
They were concerned with the administration of the palace.

They belonged to one of the three important palace associations:

#### Iwebo
- Cared for the Oba's regalia
- Supervised the craftsmen
- Conducted negotiations with European traders visiting Benin.

#### Ibiwe
- Cared for the oba's wives and children

#### Iweguae
- They provided the Oba's domestic staff of officials, cooks, servants and pages.

### 3) The Town Chiefs -

They rose to position by own efforts not by inherited wealth or connections.

They were responsible for running the various territory of the kingdom.

They collected taxes for the Oba.

They conscripted soldiers.

They mediated between village and royal interests.

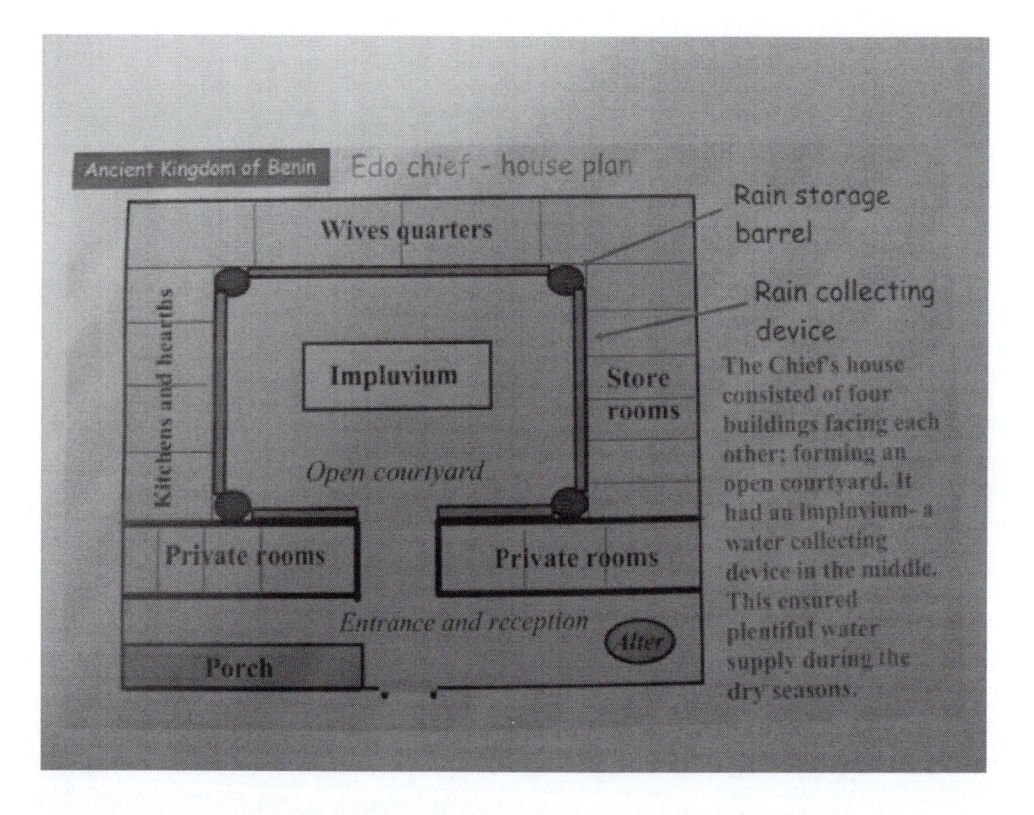

**Ancient Kingdom of Benin — Edo chief - house plan**

- Wives quarters
- Kitchens and hearths
- Impluvium
- Store rooms
- Open courtyard
- Private rooms
- Private rooms
- Entrance and reception
- Alter
- Porch
- Rain storage barrel
- Rain collecting device

The Chief's house consisted of four buildings facing each other; forming an open courtyard. It had an Impluvium - a water collecting device in the middle. This ensured plentiful water supply during the dry seasons.

Activity: Imagine that you were one of the Oba's chiefs; make a diary entry of a day in your life.

# Modern day Chief Swearing-in Ceremony in pictures

The court officials assemble for the ceremony to begin. Can you see the priestess in red? What do you think her duties are?

Notice the chief's wives hairstyles.

The whole community gathers. The musicians are in place ready to make music. (1996).

The ceremony begins.

The Enogie (local Oba) arrives for the ceremony. Notice his regalia.

The Chiefs wives are cleansed as part of the ceremony. Notice the purified white chalk marks.

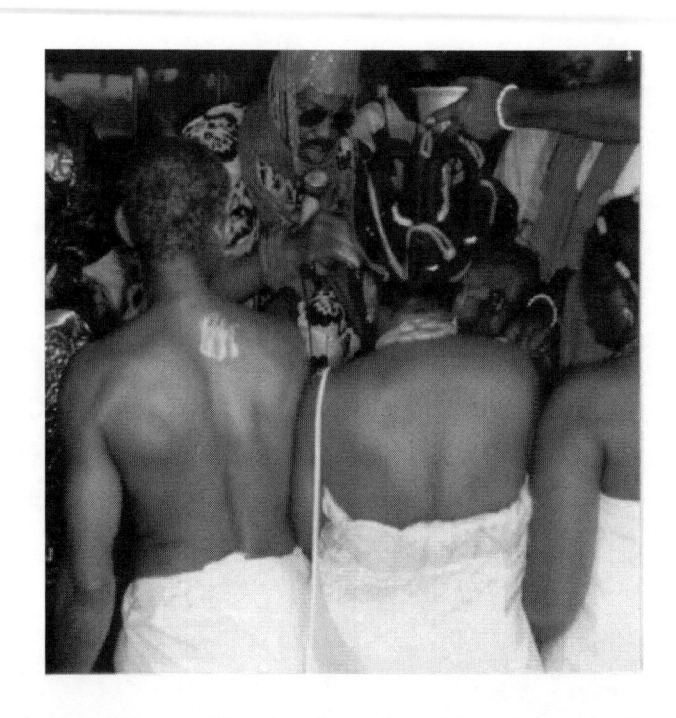

First the wives swear an oath of support for the chief's position.

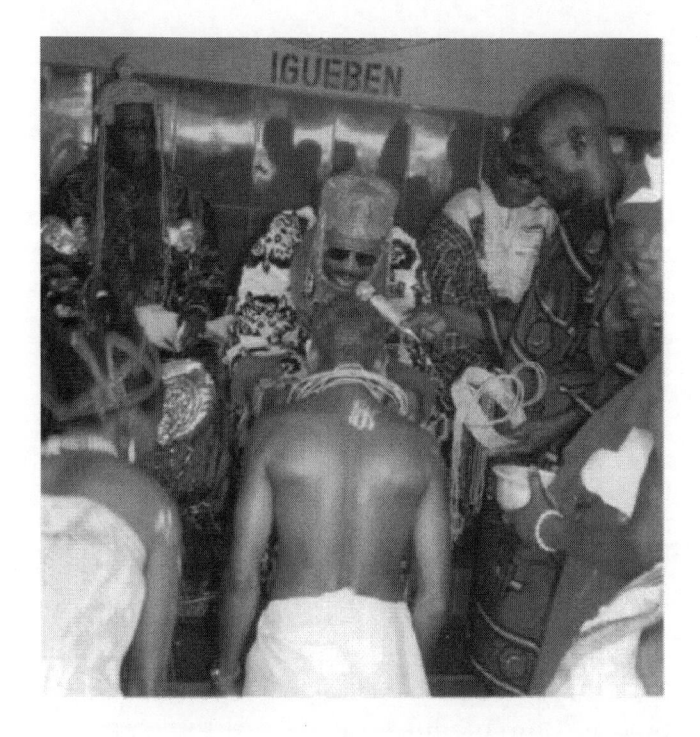

The chief then swears an oath and receives his ceremonial necklace.

Next he receives his ceremonial crown.

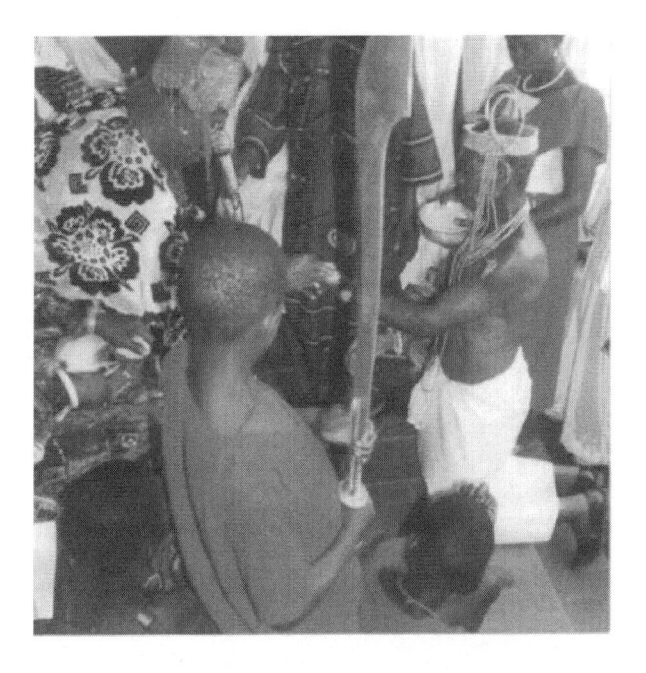

The Enogie cleanses the chief.

Finally the chief receives his sword of office.

Ceremonial Emblems

Eben - is the official symbol of authority handed over to the chief by the king.

Ada - the symbol of the higher authority possessed by the king. He alone has the authority to execute a capital offender.

Enogie of Igueben in sitting (the Ada Bearer in front of him).

The Ebenze of Igueben goes on a walkabout, the drummers in the background, still making music.

Conferment of chieftaincy title now complete, it is time for community celebration.

Chief sits with his Eben in front of him. This is his emblem of authority. Chief is now part of the council that meet regularly with the Enogie and sometimes with the Oba's council to discuss issues that affect the people and ongoing preservation of Edo culture.

Early 19th century Oba of Benin

Current Oba of Benin

# Death and Burial

Just like the Egyptians, Edos believed in *Afterlife:* that the soul rejoined the body after burial.

When an Oba died, he was buried in his full royal regalia and with an entourage to help establish his new kingdom and to take care of his every need. Believed to be essential were a band of slaves to serve him and a wife to cook for him. The slaves were buried first, then the wife and finally the Oba placed on top them to show his importance and authority.

## Succession

The first born son of the Oba was always the heir and since he was allowed many wives, several sons were produced, this caused rivalry and made it difficult to tell who was really first born. To get round this problem, potential rivals were sent to the countryside as hereditary rulers (Enogie) over administrative districts.

An elaborate ceremony described below follows interment; the same order was and is still observed for the king as his chiefs.

## A royal Chief burial ceremony

The Edos in history have always had elaborate rituals to ensure smooth transition of the deceased between the tangible world and the spiritual realm. The Chiefs and elders who are the principal custodians of Edo customs and traditions defend these practices rigorously particularly in relation to the Royal families. The only change over time is a full court is no longer buried with the King.

*When a chief dies, this is kept secret until all the village chiefs, elders and his first born son have been informed and gathered. They then carry out secret rituals behind closed doors and agree course of events over the coming days and months.*

*Cannon shots are used to announce the passing away of the chief.*

*From now on, the elders hold planning meetings regularly on the burial ceremony procedures. The wives go into mourning. They wear black clothes and cannot attend public gatherings like market or parties for three months. They are allocated companions for this period.*

When initial ceremonies have been completed cannon shots are fired again to announce commencement of chief's interment and again at the end.

The shots fired must be in odd numbers 3, 5, 7, 9, 11. Same number of shots is fired each time in a particular ceremony. The village Chiefs, elders and first born sons must decide this at the initial planning stages.

The traditional burial ceremony can last from one to five days. In the past it lasted seven days.

During the course of the celebration, the family feed the whole community who join in various activities during the day. Each day, this involves slaughtering some cows and goats and cooking cauldrons of rice and pounded yam are cooked. Crates of drinks which must not run out during the ceremony are also supplied.

Day 1:

*Early morning on Day 1 Cannon shots wake the people up* to announce the beginning of the ceremonies.

Today, there is an all night celebration of Chief's life. The community join with the children to eat, drink and dance all night long.

The wives do not join in the celebration as they are in mourning.

## Cannon shots

11 cannon shots are fired each time there is change of events and activities or someone important arrives.

The number of cannon shots has to be odd number, i.e. 3, 5, 7, 9 or 11.

The family decides how many will be fired each day during the course of the ceremony and this depends on their funds.

After the cannon shots, the Chiefs and village elders begin to gather for the day's events and ceremony.

They are in charge of the ceremonies and work hand in hand with the sons and family members on the procedures and rituals.

Punctuality is essential as the ceremonies cannot begin until every chief and elder has arrived.

The drinks must be kept flowing, the host must keep filling the crates and keep up with the kola nuts supply.

The village women elders sit away from the men. They have no say in the procedures.

Days 2 and 3
Various celebration events like masquerades entertaining the community; lots of feasting takes place with the community singing and dancing. General merriment is the order of the day.

In ancient practice, a bronze horn blower was part of the music band to entertain.

Day 4
All the married daughters are expected to come back from whichever part of the world they live in; to ensure their father gives them that final blessing before he proceeds to the spirit world. They bring various gifts to the elders to intercede on their behalf to ensure that this happens. The elders receive the gifts and pray for them.

A moderator is appointed and all negotiations are done through him. Items value could be translated into monetary terms, if this is more convenient.

The chiefs agree a levy based on factors like how often this child visits home and their past contributions to the family. The less prominent the child has been, the higher the levy. The Moderator must step in to challenge all excessive levies; he must on behalf of each daughter, put the first offer on the table. The chiefs can reject this until an acceptable offer is reached.

List of levy items
- Kola nuts
- Kegs of palm wine
- Kegs of palm kernal
- A bale of traditional African fabric
- Goats
- A bundle of yams
- Money (could be exuberant)

Day 5
Today is the last day of the ceremonies; the deceased properties will be shared out to only 1st born male offsprings

Cannon shots wake people up.

- ✓ The chiefs and village elders gather
- ✓ Masquerades entertain the guests
- ✓ All other rituals are completed today
- ✓ Food and drinks are still flowing.

The issue for the assembly is whether the deceased owed anyone, after that the sons are allocated their inheritance. They could share this with others at a later date.

Each son slaughters a cow which the elders share among themselves; this being the last tribute.

The chiefs and elders have made a lot of money from their own shares of the various levies they have imposed on the children and family.

The burial ceremonies not only celebrate the chief's life, it also provides for a continuity of Edo traditions passed on in every fine point from generation to generation. As custodians of Edo cultures and traditions, during the ceremonies, the elders have:

- been accorded respect
- earned some income from the ceremonies
- received gifts during the period
- topped up on their food supply
- safeguarded the customs

# Trade and Commerce

The Edos were very skilled carvers and blacksmiths, some of their bronze and terra cotta sculptures survive in very good state to this day.

They had extensive trade links and were known to be shrewd traders. Their style was one of rigorous negotiations and would only agree to a deal on their own terms. This meant that occasionally they negotiated for days, weeks or even months before sealing an agreement. It was therefore not an easy task to trade with them but there was always lots of profits to be made when this was successful.

The Edo traded with neighbouring nations as well as with other African Kingdoms who came from South, East and North Africa on horsebacks or by long treks. Crops traded included local produce like yams, beans, rice, gourds, cattle, sheep, goats, poultry, cotton, peanuts, sweet potatoes, cassava, vegetables and various fruit like paupua, mango, tangerines, oranges, coconut, bananas, plantain, and maize. They were also good suppliers of rubber from the rainforest.

On sea, the Edo traded with the Dutch and the Portuguese traders. Jewellery was a popular trade item. The Edos specialised in woven striped garments that were popular on the Gold Coast, blue fabric, pepper, jasper stones, and leopard skins. In exchange, they received Coral beads, red and silver fabrics - cotton, red velvet, embroidered silk, coarse flannel - candied oranges and lemons, mirrors, and iron bars.

The Edos did not use coins as money but cowrie shells which was introduced from East Africa in local trading and bronze manillas for trading with the Europeans. These are sometimes referred to as bronze bracelet money.

Cowrie shells were used as trading currency with local people.

Ivory Salt cellar. 'Afro-Portuguese ivories'.

# Religion

The people of Benin just like in Greek mythology believed in many gods and goddesses.

They viewed the world at two levels, the spirit world and the human world and to them there was no clear boundaries between these. Also as in Greek mythology, the gods and spirits daily intervene in the lives of humans, powerful humans are said to draw upon the forces of the spirit world to give them supernatural powers to transform their daily experience (supernatural beings).

The Edos also held strong beliefs in spirits, magic, and the power of witch doctors.

The Oba was believed to have mystical powers.

The Oba's motif represents him with mudfish legs.
The motif represented the people's belief in the Oba's spiritual power to be able to bridge the physical tangible world realm to the

spiritual world of the gods. For just like the mudfish that can live on both water and land, the king can switch easily between the physical world realm and the gods' spiritual realm.

## The gods hierarchy:

**Osanobua - is the creator god, the high god who lives in** magnificent palace, surrounded by courtiers and served by other deities. He is the father of other gods and assigns responsibilities of care for aspects of the world to them. He deals mainly with the spirit world and does not interfere with the running of the tangible world. He is appealed to only as a last resort, when all else has failed. He is utterly benevolent.

**Olokun** - is the first born son of Osanobua.
Responsibilities include the great oceans of the earth which surround the land and into which all the rivers flow. He is the provider of children to the Edo people, in particular beautiful women; he is therefore the god of beauty. He is the source of riches and good fortune. Exceptionally beautiful women are said to have been sent to earth by Olokun as his special devotees they kept a shrine and were priestess' to him.

Olokun's symbolic colour is white to show that he is a 'cool' god who, like his father represents the positive aspects of experiences: ritual purity, good luck, health, long life, prosperity and happiness.

**Ogiuwu:** Osanobua's other son is the god of the underworld, said to be bringer of death. He sends his messenger **Ofoe** (who is represented in Bini art as having only legs and arms) to earth to take human life. He chases his victims with his legs and catches them with his arms for return to Ogiuwu. Being a bad guy he is no longer prominent in Benin religious worship.

**Ogiuwu's** symbolic colour is black.

**Ogun** is Osanobua's junior son is patron of farmers, craftsmen, hunters, and warriors (all those who depend on tools). He was sent to the world to make farm and to make war. Ogun's devotees are protected by him and he uses his sword to open the way to a better life for them. They are thus progressive people.

The ceremonial swords the *eben and the ada* represent Ogun's powers as metallic objects of indestructibility. The Oba is said to be indestructible.

Ogun's symbolic colour is red which depicts sudden and violent actions, e.g. thunderstorm, fire, blood.

**Osun-** is god of the rainforest. He is said to reside in the leaves and herbs of the forest. Like his brother Ogun, he is concerned with how raw materials from the forest are processed and transformed into instruments of power which preserve and maintain life on earth.

His symbolic colour is red.

## Religious festivals

The Edos celebrated lots of annual festivals in honour of their various gods and goddesses. The Oba led these ceremonies and wore ceremonial robes during these periods. He always carried a sword *the eben*, which was a symbol of his authority. There were many festivals including new yam harvest festivals to honour the gods, Ogun and Osun. All subjects had to stop work for several days to attend a festival. An example is the new yam festival which lasted for seven days and involved feasting and merry making for the whole period.

The Edos believed in work hard and play hard to achieve a healthy lifestyle.

# Art

The Oba wanted people to see him as divine and powerful and went to great length to achieve this through art. He adorned his palace with hundreds of extravagant metal plaques produced by palace blacksmiths and carvers.

This resulted in Edo becoming famous for its sculpture and art, which were exported to other parts of the world through trade and to this day remain so.

The Oba had the sole control of the brass plaque production in the Kingdom. The Edo produced brass plaques for him only and if they broke this rule, they could be put to death.

Brass was chosen as a material for plaque making because it is metal and hard and long lasting just like the Oba. It showed the power of the Oba as indestructible and everlasting.

The plaques were generally small about 46 centimetres or one and a half feet tall. They were used to record Edo's achievements.

Carved wooden door at the palace show the ada and eben and the Oba and attendants

Bronze plague showing the Oba of Benin with his attendants.
Notice the young pages. They spend years learning their jobs at the palace, today, attendants and receive a qualification and certificate certifying their position at the palace.

Queen Idia. Queen mother of Oba Esigie.

Bronze figure of a huntsman carrying an antelope with a dog at his knee. The bronze figures tell us about Edo's way of life, we can see from above that hunters used dogs to help them in hunt in the forest.

# The King's Festival

The King's festival known as Igue festival is celebrated between Christmas and New Year. It has been celebrated since the time of Oba Ewuare, one of the warrior kings who reigned in the 15th century. During the festival, the king's divinity and magical powers were renewed and he blessed his people. Foreigners and non-natives were not allowed to see the king during the festival period. It was also a great time of feasting for the people.

Here its celebration is presented in the form of palace news:

## **This Year's Igue Festival**

Here are some things you need to remember throughout the 9 days festival:

1. The reason you have not seen His Majesty and some of his chiefs for some days now is that they have been preparing for the Igue festival by completing the Agwe (fasting). So when you see them for the first time on the first day, you need to cheer at the top of your vocal cords. Your cheerful noise will encourage and reassure them that they have your full support as a people.

2. Remember that unless you are a chief, you must arrive early each day to get a good spot to watch the celebration from; otherwise you will not be able to see a thing. Try to get out of bed as soon as the cock crows, have a proper bath, adorn yourself in your finest attire and jewellery, have a good meal and head straight for the palace to secure your space.

3. If you are accompanying a chief as part of his entourage, remember to get his own programme the day before otherwise, you will find that you have been pushed out of your role and limelight; it is after all a great honour to be accompanying a chief to these celebrations.

4. Remember to be on your best behaviour, no offhand comment and cheer as loudly as you can for every single activity by the Oba

or his chiefs. You are there to show your support for His Majesty and his great Chiefs, so do so very enthusiastically.

5. Have a good rest each night so you are refreshed for the next day's activities and events.

6. Make sure that you manage to visit all chiefs' and other people's houses for some feasting and dancing and take care to make your presence felt, lavishing praises on their wives and children when they take the dance floor will not go unnoticed. You might be invited to join one of the youth clubs after this.

7. Remember that the festival is a time for observing our religious rituals as well as a time for merry making, feasting, wining, dining and dancing. It is very important to enjoy yourself.

8. Plan how you will use the nine days fruitfully to gain the most from all the generosity people will be showing. This means make the most of it or you could miss out on a freebee. The Chiefs normally give out souvenirs like wooden Ise game boards carved in their images on it; you could also collect some free spending money they give out as tips or when you get 'showered' during your dance. Be creative and use your full imagination during the nine days!

## **Programme of Events**

**Day 1:** His Majesty dresses in his ceremonial robes and sits on the royal throne. His High ranking chiefs led by the Iyase (the Prime Minister) pay homage to him by dancing with their Eben emblem. The Ubi ritual of wading off evil spirits takes place. The Oba blesses all the homes in the kingdom through the Ewere. The Oba and his chiefs pay homage at our ancestral shrines.

**Day 2:** Ritual day. The Efas (the blessings priests) sanctify His Majesty with white chalk on his forehead. His Majesty blesses the sacrificial items. The high priest the Isekhure cleanses and slaughters the animals in a special ritual. His Majesty, his chiefs and members of the palace societies are anointed.

**Day 3:** Members of the Royal family, the Princes and Princesses dance to honour His Majesty and the kingdom.

**Day 4:** Free day for community celebrations and activities like masquerades, Feasting, dining and lots of dancing. Groups of friends and family members visit each other's houses to enjoy the feast each household has prepared. Spend all day in merriment, feasting and dancing.

**Day 5:** Free day for community celebrations and activities like masquerades, Feasting, dining and lots of dancing. Groups of friends and family members visit each other's houses to enjoy the feast each household has prepared. Spend all day in merriment, feasting and dancing. Visit the houses you haven't yet.

**Day 6:** Edo people – the whole community celebrate and visit and dance for the Oba to honour him.

**Day 7:** Free day for community celebrations and activities like masquerades, Feasting, dining and lots of dancing. Groups of friends and family members visit each other's houses to enjoy the feast each household has prepared. Spend all day in merriment, feasting and dancing. Visit the houses you haven't yet.

**Day 8:** Free day for community celebrations and activities like masquerades, Feasting, dining and lots of dancing. Groups of friends and family members visit each other's houses to enjoy the feast each household has prepared. Spend all day in merriment, feasting and dancing. Visit the houses you haven't yet.

**Day 9:** Last day of celebration, by now you should have visited all houses and joined in their celebration and feasting. Remember no one should be left out, check that you have seen everyone, we are one unit this festival time; we eat from the same pot and drink from the same keg. The Enogies (Outskirts rulers) must now set their own dates for celebrating their festival in the same fashion back in their domain. These will be around the New Year.

**Remember that there should be no burial ceremony taking place during the festival period.**

Please ensure that you have prepared well in advance for the events.

Have fun!

It was and still is a great time of feasting and celebration for the community.

# Slavery

The Edos acquired slaves for debt recovery purposes or insolvency, avenging maltreatment or captured in war. In some cases slaves were born into slavery. The Edos did not engage in buying and selling of slaves like other Kingdoms and nations. Maltreating a slave was not part of the Edo culture.

The slave children had the same experiences as the household children except that if a slave child had something the other child wanted, s/he had to give it up and in some households had to be served food last. Slave children did most of the work the other children refused to do. They joined in games and other activities when they were not working.

Slave girls after a long service sometimes became one of the many wives of house master. Slave boys who worked out their time gained their freedom; they could also marry into the household and become family members enjoying privileges of the family.

This meant that slaves could buy their freedom by paying their master the price of their purpose or by marrying into the household.

# Food

Most Edo people were farmers and grew their own food. Children were taught to farm from a very early age. As people were busy farming or doing other jobs during the day, the Edo meal consisted of one large meal in the evening. Here is a typical Edo daily meal:

Breakfast:
- Roasted plantain or corn with fruit

Lunch:
- Light meal e.g. cassava garri with meat or fish with friut
- Roasted yam or plantain with palm oil and fruit

Dinner:
- Feast of Pounded yam or yam and cassava (fou-Fou) fill up with eba (cassava paste).
- Vegetable soup with fresh and dry meat, bushmeat, snails, crayfish and fresh or dry fish.
- More fruit and vegetables; washed down with spring water and palm wine for the men.

Young children preferred the sweet plantain or sweet potato and fruit to pounded yam.

Rice meal was a treat or reserved for celebration days.

**Festive food:**
During festive seasons, the Edo sent food gifts to friends, family and the nobles. This included game meat, goats, chickens, fish, bundles of yams and kegs of palm wine and occasionally bundles of corn head. The generosity of the sender depended on how wealthy he was, in this case how fruitful his harvest has been, therefore the more food gifts they gave out, the more highly they were regarded by others.

During these festive days, known as Ukpe, Edos woke up at the crack of dawn to prepare cauldrons of food. Part of this they sent to neighbours, families and friends as token of good wishes, the remaining was served throughout the day to visitors, who came in mainly to wine and dine. Everyone went into each other's house and ate as much as they wanted as the whole community becomes one. During the day, all households maintained an open door policy and were not expected to run out of food.

This cooking, wining and dining as a single community unit continued for the five days of celebration.

**Festive food list:**
Kola nuts
- Yam - Boiled or pounded
- Cassava: as garri or mixed with pounded yam.
- Cocoyam pounded with yam, when this is in short supply
- Corn and Maize Roasted of ground
- Dried beans for making akara, mai-mai, etc
- Vegetables for soup making e.g. Egusi (melon seeds), ogbono, okra, spinach, water leaf, bitter leaf, nut meg, pepper,
- Fruit e.g. Mango, paw-paw, oranges, tangerines, cashew, guava, forest berries
- Meat- bush meat, antelopes, boars, pork, chicken, cows. goats, sheep,
- Fish- Fresh and dried or smoked.
- Drinks - Palm wine, coconut drink, local gin, spring water.

Rich households had more visitors than others and had to provide more food than others. Some used up to ten cows, twenty four goats, fifty chickens and countless games for cooking during the festive season (five days).

Activity: Try out a couple of the recipes in the resources section. Remember Edos did not use knives and forks to eat. You must use your fingers.

# End of Old Kingdom
## The end of an era

The kingdom of Benin began to decline with events elsewhere especially in Europe. It was hastened with the coming of the British who were out to expand their protectorates in Africa. They saw Edos as a hindrance to their advancement into the interiors of Africa and when a dispute broke out about the signing over of the kingdom to the British, they were quick to send in a punitive expedition, which burnt down and looted the royal palace and major buildings in Benin City thus ending the era of a powerful and progressive Rainforest Kingdom.

## Sequence of events

**Who was involved in The Benin Massacre of 1897:**

**1892** Oba Ovonramwen - tricked into signing protectorate treaty by Henry Gallwey.

Dispute breaks out about terms and intents of the treaty. Oba Ovonramwen bars all British officials and traders from entering Benin territories.

**March 1896** - Oba Ovonramwen closes all trade routes along the coast, puts a trade embargo in place. The British are unhappy.

**December 1896** - Consul Philips - violates Edo's custom. Insists and enters the Kingdom during an important religious festival for sons of the land only (the five-day Igue festival). This despite repeated advice from the king to wait till after the festival.

Chief Ologboshere and other chiefs - demand atonement to appease the gods.

Chief Ologboshere and selected soldiers from the Edo skilled army force are sent to the border at Gwato to stop Consul Philip entering the kingdom and disturbing the festival.

There is a dispute about what happened next but on:

**4th January 1897** - four white men including Captain Philips and his 250 African attendants are killed as they forcefully try to enter the kingdom. Two White men escape by hiding in the forest.

**January 12 1897** - the British form the Benin Punitive expedition to capture the king and destroy Benin City.

**February 9 1897** - The British declare war. Benin soldiers defend their city fiercely and pluckily, a British battalion is routed and its commander beheaded. The war continues for ten days.

**19th February** - British troupes seize Benin

**Between 19th and 21st February** - British troupes shell Benin City setting it ablaze. They march through the city with firearms, shooting everything in sight. They burn down and loot the palace and senior chiefs' houses; they kill some high ranking chiefs.

With their city burnt down, the Edo people flee into neighbouring villages.

**August 1897** - Oba Ovonramwen surrenders.

**September 1897** - Queen Victoria's chief agent, Consul-General Ralph Moore tries Oba Ovonramwen and his remaining chiefs. He sentences Chief Ologboshere and three other chiefs to death. They are hanged.

Oba Ovonramwen is exiled to Calabar.

Without a ruler, Edo people lose their will and surrender to British rule.

**Late 1897** - looted artworks from Benin are auctioned in Paris, France. They eventually, end up in private collections and museums across the world.

**Oba Ovonramwen dies in 1914** whilst on exile in Calabar.

The British restore the crown returning ceased royal regalia.

**Prince Aiguobasimwin** is crowned as **Oba Eweka 11**.

Oba Eweka 11 rebuilds the palace in its current site though on a much smaller scale than the old palace.

A new era begins for the Edo people.

Oba Ovonramwen (1888 – 1914) last king of the old kingdom

# Modern Benin

King Eweka 11, the Lion-heart was a very well educated king who used his diplomatic skills to persuade the British to restore the Benin monarchy. His argument was that the Edo monarchy was on par with the British and once his request was granted, he set about rebuilding the royal palace. He was also a very skilled and accomplished carver and blacksmith. Using these skills he built the palace which is occupied by the present Oba of Benin.

**The Benin traditional institution has since changed in a number of ways including:**

The Elected governor of Edo state must approve any crowned royal before he is given the official staff of office.

The Elected governor of Edo state has the power to remove a king.

Submission to a monarch's jurisdiction is optional although the local people rarely go against it.

The Courts have the overall say in jurisdiction matters.

The District Enogies and Chiefs have also had to adapt to changing times e.g. after being crowned traditionally, they still seek the recognition of the elected governor and in judicial matters submit to the courts.

The Oba of Benin in sitting. Make a sketch drawing of one of the personal attendants.

His Majesty Erediauwa 1

Oba of Benin

Omo'N'Oba

The supreme ruler of the Edo people

Current king of Benin Kingdom

Statues in Benin City

House of Assembly meeting

Oba Akenzua 11 2nd King in new Era

Edo warrior

# Glossary

## Benin Background page

Ancient - a long time ago

Chieftaincy - high ranking official

Customs - people's way of life

Divine - being or having the nature of a god

Forest Kingdom - a forest area that were ruled by a local king

Heir - successor: a person who inherits some title or office

Oral traditions - passed down from generation to generation by word of mouth.

Shrine - An altar or niche dedicated to a particular Goddess or God and held to be sacred.

Virtue - the quality of doing what is right and avoiding what is wrong

## Modern Chief Swearing in ceremony page

Conferment - bestowal: the act of conferring an honour

Descendants - Ones Children, Grandchildren, Great-grandchildren, etc.

Mediated - acting or brought about through an intervening agency

Official - a worker who holds or is invested with an office

Political elite - A small group of people with a disproportionate amount of public decision-making power.

Terra cotta - Fired clay (literally 'baked earth')

## Childhood page

Commerce - trade or exchange of goods and money.

Crop preservation - the activity of protecting the yield from plants in a single growing season from loss or danger

Drought - a prolonged period of dryness that can cause damage to plants.

Games - animals hunted for food or sport.

Produce - fresh fruits and vegetable grown for the market.

## Trade and Commerce page

Blacksmith - A crafter of iron and steel.

Coral beads - Beads made from the hard stony skeleton of a Mediterranean coral that has a delicate red or pink colour

Cowrie shells - marine snails of the genus Cypraea (family Cypraeidae), found chiefly in tropical regions, especially around the Maldives or the East Indies. The shell itself is smooth and more or less egg-shaped, with a long, narrow, slit-like opening (aperture).

Dialects - a particular version of a language with its own distinctive accent, grammar and vocabulary.

Rural - sparsely settled places away from the influence of large cities and towns

Suitor - a man who courts a woman


## Slavery page

Acquire - get: come into the possession of something concrete or abstract.

Insolvency - The inability of an individual or entity to pay its debts when they are due.

Maltreat - mistreat: treat badly.

Slave - a person who is owned by someone.

Privilege - a special advantage or immunity or benefit not enjoyed by all.


## Religion page

Alter - a special surface or place set aside for magical workings and/or religious acknowledgement

Benevolent - generous in providing aid to others

Deities - or gods held in high regard and worshipped by human beings

Devotees - people who worship the god regularly

Mythology - Old stories that usually explain how something came to be

Priestess - woman who takes an officiating role in worship of any religion

Supernatural - Something that cannot be given an ordinary explanation

## Art page

Brass - A yellowish alloy consisting mainly of copper and zinc

Ceremonies - a set of activities, infused with ritual significance and performed on certain occasions

Festivals - a set of celebrations in the honour of a god

Patron - someone who supports or favours some person, group, or institution

Underworld - in Classical mythology, this is the land of shadows where souls of the dead have to pass through to get to heaven or hell

Plaque - brass: a memorial made of brass

## The end of an era page

Protectorate - a state or territory controlled by a more powerful state

Decline - change toward something smaller or lower

Hindrance - the act of hindering or obstructing or impeding

Punitive expedition - the military excursion sent by the British in 1897; which totally destroyed the sophisticated West African kingdom of Benin

Massacre - kill a large number of people indiscriminately

Treaty - written agreement between two states or sovereigns

Appease - make peace with

Atonement - compensation for a wrong

Consul - a representative of a foreign government

Exiled - to be sent away from one's home (city, state or country) while either being explicitly refused permission to return and/or being threatened by prison or death upon return

Loot - plunder: steal goods; take as spoils

Routed - direction diverted

# Brain teasers

History quiz:

When and where was the Kingdom of Benin?
Who were the Binis?
Kings of Benin timeline
What was childhood like?
What gods did they worship and why?
What food did they eat?
What food did they eat?
What jobs did the people do?
What goods did they trade and with whom?
Why did the Kingdom of Benin end/ collapse?
What was the scramble for Africa?

Geography quiz:
Where was/ is Benin in the world?
What is the climate in Benin like?
What is the weather like?
What is the population of Benin?
What languages do the people speak?
Does Benin have a monarchy and why?

# Inside A Rainforest Royal Court

## Growing up In Benin: 2

*Fidelia Nimmons*

Preface

Great Kingdom of Benin was probably the greatest Kingdom to exist in West Africa. Things changed with European colonisation of Africa in the 19th century. Its story however continues to intrigue and excite scholars and historians alike.

The kingdom's people hold fast to their ancestral customs, adapting when they need to e.g. in embracing Christianity and modern influences from other countries and cultures particularly the West.

This volume looks at aspects of life for the ordinary people of the kingdom; volume one covers palace life focusing on the king and his chiefs presenting information on aspects of palace life such as Government, Trade and Commerce and Art.

How to use:
This book is to be read in conjunction with volume one: *Inside A Rainforest Royal Court: Kingdom of Benin.*

Some sections are written in present tense because there has been so little change in that aspect of Edo culture. Past and current practices are exactly the same; example is the traditional marriage ceremony.

Photographs included are for present day practices which have not changed much since ancient times e.g. the Market.

You will find a glossary at the end of the book which explains specialist words written in red throughout the book.

Words in the glossary are grouped according to the section where they are used.

Activities ideas are included for those wanting the Benin or Edo experience.

A list of websites for further reading is included at the back of the book.


Fidelia Nimmons

# Contents

| | |
|---|---|
| Edo Calendar and Seasons | 64 |
| Social structure | 66 |
| Childhood | 70 |
| Palace apprenticeship | 76 |
| Marriage | 78 |
| Edo Market | 85 |
| Illness and Health | 89 |
| Edo recipes | 91 |
| Oral Stories | 94 |
| Activities and games | 99 |
| Glossary | 108 |
| Further reading | 110 |

# Edo Calendar and Seasons

Edo astronomers used a combination of Lunar and solar calendar systems to map their seasons, year and months. This is called the Lunisolar calendar system.

<u>Edo calendar month</u>

Edo astronomers based this on the lunar system using their knowledge of motion time of the moon around the earth. In the 28 days it takes the moon to make a complete orbit around the sun, Edo astronomers identified seven phases of the moon during the complete orbit (Over time other world astronomers increased this to nine.). Using this knowledge, they calculated their week as four days. They then used this figure to calculate the length of their month resulting in seven weeks (of four days each) in Edo calendar month.

Below is Edo Lunar calendar:

> **Market day is four days**
> **Uzala is one week**
> **One moon (Uki) is one month**
> **Ukpo (one complete seasonal cycle) is one year.**

<u>Edo calendar seasons</u>

Edo astronomers used the solar or tropical calendar to calculate their seasons and year. These were based on the two tropical:

1. Raining season
2. Dry season

They combined their knowledge of their farmers' land use with that of the seasons to plan schedule of events based on farming and achieving a rich harvest.

Festivals and other celebrations were marked during the dry seasons when they were not likely to be washed out by torrential rains or when people were busy on their farms. Example is the king's festival - *Igue*

Edo seasons and months can be matched to the universal calendar months as below:

> **February /March are farming land clearing season (preparing for sowing farming plots).**
> *April / May are planting season*
> **June / July / August are the raining season**
> *September/ October are the harvest season*
> **November / December/ January are the dry and cold season (harmattan) during this time, farming land lie fallow.**

Timing the day

Edo used the position of the sun in the sky to organise their day. Events were planned to take account of weather hotness throughout the day.

Using the position of the sun in the sky as clock, farmers did their hard labour before mid day and took a break when the day was at its hottest. Community meetings were held in the cool evenings

Edo used position of the sun in the sky to structure their day.

# Social structure

Benin Kingdom social structure was based on seniority and personal achievements. The social group one belonged to dictated responsibility and respect one got from others.

Women and children

Women were generally home makers.

**Older women**'s duties included being head of their household; maintaining, painting and decorating their homes; renovating family alters, cleaning and polishing alter items. They earned income through farming or trading and were responsible for the well being of their entire household. Where a man had several wives, the senior wife acted as the household manager and overseer.

A modern village market scene.

Women and maidens owned most of the stalls. Children and women did the buying and selling of perishable goods. Men sold produce like yams, fabric and furniture items.

**Maidens** were the main workers of the household. They helped to educate the younger children on house chores e.g. fetching water and collecting firewood from the forest. They acted as group leaders when out and about with groups of children. It was their duty to ensure storerooms were stacked full with food including sacks of grains like corn and maize and bundles of yams. They dried bush meat and fish and did most of the cooking; serving food to each and every member of the family. They sold perishable farm produce they did not need such as vegetables in the weekly market.

**Younger children** were the errand bearers and had to take instructions from others senior to them. They looked after the family livestock like cows, goats and chickens. They cleaned the house and fetched water and firewood under the guidance of the older siblings. It was also their job to show foreign visitors round town. The market was a must see attraction for all visitors.

## Men

The king and his chiefs were at the top of the social structure; they legislated and ensured that the kingdom ran smoothly.

Other men in the kingdom were divided into 4 groups or classes; each with its own unique feature and responsibilities within the kingdom.

The Ancient Kingdom of Benin social structure is still in place today and is described below:

At the top were the **Odionweres**. They were second in command next to the Enogie (local King) and acted in their absence. They led meetings of the elders and seniors in the **Oguedion**, their meeting place. They had real power and had to be listened to.

Odionweres and Edions were the most senior.

**Edion** were the next most important people, they met in the Oguedion (House of the seniors or elders). Aged 65 years and over, they were initiated into the group for their life valuable experiences or as younger men with religious responsibilities. They met regularly to decide on affairs such as traditional customs or on schedule and arrangements for upcoming annual festivals. An example is they planned schedule of events for the King's Igue festival; they decided order of events for each day of the festival e.g. when each chief should dance before the king to honour him. This was a delegated responsibility from the King and they kept him informed of decisions taken.

**Eghele**. Aged between 18 and 40 years and over, they were the order keepers in the community. Since they were in their prime years, they were family men who carried out chores like farming, keeping the community safe from outside threats and were the warriors who fought the kingdoms wars. Their duties included ensuring that every member of the community could participate in the upcoming Igue festival by distributing food, meat and other celebration items to households who would otherwise not have enough. They maintained the community welfare system so no one had to go without whilst some others had abundant harvest.

**Ikpolo Ughe.** Aged from 7 to 18 years, this group of young men kept the town clean. They dug wells, swept roads, made new roads and pruned overgrown trees. Quite simply they were the city's health inspectors and workers; periodically, a work schedule was agreed by the group led by their leader who called them out and kept an eye on the quality of their work. Failure to turn up for community work led to sanctions and fines including paying the cost of a livestock. This system is still used today.

# Childhood

Childhood for Edo children was a time of great enjoyment, discovery and fun. From well preserved ways of life, stories, songs, children's plays and books, we can get a good idea of what growing up in the Kingdom of Benin was like.

Edo children liked to look good and beautiful; they liked to please Olokun, the god of beauty and the bringer of good luck; they therefore took great care to look good and beautiful. The Edos have retained this aspect of their culture well over time. They continue to use red coral jewellery to adorn themselves in order to look beautiful and as a way to celebrate their rich culture.

### **Education:**

Children did not go to school in a building but instead were taught at home by their parents and the extended family which included grandparents, uncles, aunts and other distant relatives. Proverbs and stories were the main teaching tools. Edo children learned the trades of their parents.

## BOYS

Boys were taught their father's trade e.g. blacksmithing, wood carving, traditional doctors, and builders so they could become main providers when they married or their fathers died. If their fathers had more than one wife they inherited all the wives not related to them. A boy could become head of the family at any age.

An Edo boy was taught to hunt for games in the rain forest. They hunted and killed games like deer, elephant, bush rats, antelopes, boars, birds, etc. they also fished for all kinds of fish, shrimps, crabs etc.

Along with their parents, boys farmed during the raining period and harvested the crops in the dry season. Their produce was either for home consumption or for commerce. They also learnt the art of crop preservation for drought seasons.

Boys learned how to farm and grow food

Other learning activities for boys included taking part in construction and building works e.g. on houses and farm barns, well digging etc.

During festive periods they practiced in secrecy for masquerading (spirits coming out among the living) and learned sophisticated singing and dancing moves to present these.

An Edo boy's life growing up was very busy and full of fun. By the time he was old enough to get married, he had already acquired so many skills he could be successful in any trade of his choice.

GIRLS

Girls were taught household skills like cleaning the house and cooking from very early age. Their duties included, fetching water from rivers, lakes and streams for which they sometimes travelled miles. Because these trips were very far away they usually went in groups and told themselves stories and jokes on the way. They also made up songs which they practiced graceful dance moves for (very useful for when a suitor comes round). They carried their water in calabash gourds which they balanced on their heads with pieces of cloth or palm leaves.

Wood carving of girl carrying calabash

Girls along with their mothers were responsible for going to the market, cooking, washing and cleaning. Their other duties included keeping the fire places clean and well stocked by fetching woods from the forest.

Preparing pounded yam

Girls learnt to paint mud jugs etc, to weave and sew and most important of all to plait or braid hair. They once a year sold articles they have made, cooked, or farmed at a large make believe market where the currency was mainly cowry shells. Industrious girls who made lots of profits were allowed to keep this and save for future use.

Girls learn to braid hair from a very early age

### In the evening / night time

After the day's work was done, Edo children had fun at night; the following included some of the activities they did to pass time before retiring for the night.

**Stories by moonlight:** this tradition continues in almost every part of rural village life, where adults mainly women tell younger children stories with moral themes; or stories to explain natural phenomena like why babies bring up the curd. Many of their stories have forest and sea themes; fables about ant kingdoms and consequences of encountering one of the inhabitants, teach children to leave anthills well alone and to respect other animal homes. Stories about undersea kingdoms, keep children who cannot swim away from rivers and seas so they do not drown.

Moonlight tales include fables about the ant kingdom

**Songs and rhymes:** Edo children made up many 'nonsense rhymes' with no particular meanings. These they could play lots of games with; excluding adults as they only understood the rules and meanings of the words they used. Most Edo children were competent in several dialects of the language and when the Portuguese and other Europeans arrived, in order to communicate with them, the Edo invented the pidgin form of their languages e.g. Pidgin-English, a combination of English and Edo language.

All children were allowed to keep farm animals such as rabbits, goats, chickens, fowls and pigs as pets. They took responsibilities for caring for these until they were sold to the family or at the market for a price.

The Extended family system

Childhood was fun for Edo children due to the effectiveness of the extended family system. The African adage of 'It takes s a village to raise a child;' was very true in the Benin kingdom, there was always a mum or dad, uncle or aunty, grandma or granddad around to chastise the child.

The extended family is still important to the Edo people today.

# Palace apprenticeship

Palace apprenticeship accorded training opportunities for future king's chiefs and attendants. Here is an account from the period of experiences for a typical palace apprentice:

*Odigie is Uwa's brother, the last son of Chief Irriah. Chief Irriah has four wives (most chiefs do) and 12 children in total, Uwa and Odigie are his youngest children by his youngest and most favourite wife.*

*All sons learn their fathers' trade through apprenticeship; since Chief Irriah is a palace Iwebo Chief and a grand master and respected member of the Royal Guild of Blacksmiths, his seven sons have a variety of trade they could learn including Royal Soldiers and Warriors, palace duties, heralds, blacksmithing, doctors including herbalists, seers, commodity tradesmen, wood carvers, leatherworkers, community entertainers and farming.*

*Odigie is currently in apprenticeship at the palace under his father's guidance so that he is able to eventually become an Iwebo chief. In this role, he will have responsibility for the King's regalia; manage and control all palace craftsmen along with other Iwebo chiefs; carry out negotiations with foreigner traders.*

*Other boys in chieftaincy apprenticeship roles in the palace will be training to be one of either of the other types of chiefs: The Uzama chiefs, these are direct descendants of the first Royal family and it is a heredity position; the other types of chieftaincy are the Town Chiefs who are appointed by the King as a result of their own efforts, these positions given as rewards or recognition by the king of people's personal efforts and achievements.*

*Odigie comes to the palace with his dad daily, he learns how to make and care for the king's robes and regalia and acts as one of the king's personal attendants. When the king is in sitting in court, Odigie holds one of the ceremonial emblems: the Ada- this shows the King' sole authority as the executioner and the Eben- a symbol of the king's authority to rule the people.*

*The apprentice is one of the smaller figures in this plaque*

*When Odigie is not at the palace, he works on learning to become a respectable member of the Royal Guilds of Blacksmith. This is the only group of people with patent to practice their unique craft. At other times, Odigie accompanies his dad to one of his many farms to learn husbandry skills.*

*For relaxation, Odigie and other male youths learn masquerading and other performance arts like contortionism, taking part in cross town competitions regularly. They can become local celebrities through these resulting in community leadership roles such as deciding marriage dowries for marrying couples.*

*Odigie gets the best training for his future position as one of the king's chiefs or king's attendant.*

# Marriage Ceremonies

Edo traditional marriage ceremonies have changed little since ancient times. The elders ensure all procedures are followed and as such this is one of the areas that have been perfectly preserved.

Edo traditional Marriage

When a man and woman decide they would like to spend the rest of their lives together, they both inform their families. From this stage they are no longer participants in the matter.

The first step is: the man's family, get a delegation together to seek out where the maiden comes from. They must find out, if her family is good and whether they will make good in laws. The woman's family await their prospective in laws to make a proposal of marriage. They visit at least three times to negotiate terms.

At the next stage, a moderator from the community is appointed and it is his job to mediate and negotiate favourable terms for both parties. Only men are usually involved in the negotiations.

During the actual ceremony, it is the moderator's role to relate the requests of the groom's people to the bride's father, Chief and village elders.

The moderator in action

Backstage, the women negotiate on behalf of the bride. They finalise her needs for when she joins her new family. She will need plenty of clothes, jewellery, make up and pocket money. The parties agree how much of each should be provided by the groom's family.

The chief negotiator writes down the agreed items in a list and both parties get a copy. Here is a copy below:

## Terms of agreeing to this union

- You must not maltreat her
- You must keep her well fed
- You must keep her well clothed
- She must maintain her current wellbeing
- Any sign of unhappiness will result in her return to us.

The most senior female in the bride's camp, relates terms of the agreement to the full gathering.

With terms and conditions agreed, the suitor must now pick out his intended bride from daughters of the family.

## The test of how well the groom knows his bride

To be completely convinced that the suitor knows his bride very well, he must pass the test of identifying her from her outline only. Three maidens are covered up from head to toe and paraded before him; he must pick his bride out correctly or fail the test and return home to start negotiations again.

The suitor is questioned rigorously about attributes of his bride by the women negotiators. He must answer each question correctly and then pick her out by her outline from a line of veiled maidens.

It is only after getting through this hurdle, is the marriage ceremony allowed to proceed.

## The dowry (bride price)

After the suitor has rightly identified his bride and has her with him, it remains to pay her dowry.

The suitor's family ask the moderator to find out how much the bride is worth. He negotiates on their behalf for a favourable term.

Agreed amount must be high enough to reflect skills of the bride, e.g. when the bride is a lawyer, the dowry must reflect her earning power now lost to her family and cost of educating her to such high standards of education.

The dowry must however not be too high that the suitor cannot pay. All expenditure on the ceremony so far is also taken into account.

Agreed price is handed to the moderator to pay her family.

Bridal Dress:

The bride is dressed in coral beads and expensive fabric e.g. judge.

The bride's attendant is also dressed in same material. She too is adorned with coral beads all over.

Now the bride is with her groom, she must be accompanied by her attendant and close companion at all times.

Bridegroom, bride and bride attendant

Bridegroom and bride

Showering with money

To set the bride on her way and to ensure that she has plenty of pocket money to set her up in her new life, the bride is 'showered' with money from members of her family, starting with her father.

This practice usually ensures that the bride does not immediately start asking her new family for money. It also reimburses her for any expenses on the marriage so far.

Showering of the bride by her father

Edo marriage ceremonies nowadays include Western style Christian wedding; however these are performed on different days in order to separate the two.

As such they perform and celebrate their:
1. Traditional wedding first
2. Church wedding; after completing their traditional rites.

Taken together, marriage ceremonies are quite spectacular occasions for the whole community, an occasion to showcase red coral in jewellery and clothing. See pictures above.

<u>The Church wedding</u>

The very next day after the traditional ceremonies, the bride's maids have to dress up again, this time in white wedding clothes. They are joined by the page boy, not needed in a traditional wedding.

After the church ceremony, the community dance the bride and groom into the reception grounds. Being cheerful and happy people, Edos take every opportunity to pray, sing and dance at every occasion.

When the marriage rituals are completed, it is time to sing, dance and dine. The whole community join in to wish the happy couple well.

# Edo Market

Edo markets were very much well organised and still are. Market days were planned well ahead on the year's calendar by the palace council. All chiefs took note of the dates and disseminated this information to the whole community.

Market day was a big deal for Edo people. At the crack of dawn, those with stalls went to the market square to pitch their ware, before returning home to dress up for the day so they look their best. People going only to buy items from the market; dressed up for the occasion too. Edo market was not only a place for selling and buying but was also for socialising and used as information sharing centre. This practice continues to this day.

The information below is presented in present tense because Edo Markey Day practices have hardly changed overtime.

Edo market days

These come around every four days and everyone from all corners of the city come to join in a massive get together and sharing of all manners of niceties. The market is held in special area of the city near to the palace, it is looked after by a market Chief called the Ikeki.

**The Ikeki's jobs include:**

1. Allocating spaces for pitches and stalls on a first come first served basis to all traders (equal opportunities). All families send a representative to the market at the first sight of daylight to secure a pitch or stall. Others join later looking their best in dress and make up.

2. Ensuring dedicated areas for sale and exchange of specific items and commodities.

3. Keeping everyone up to date with latest information from the palace e.g. announcements from regarding major events like the Oba's (king) festival arrangements,

4. Providing Edo citizens with information on e.g. expected foreign visitors, other major events like vaccination and inoculation against maladies like Guinea worms etc. People need to know when these will take place, where, who will be administering these and how they will arrange the day.

5. Ensuring Health and safety of all during market time e.g. a lost child can be announced immediately with a crier ringing a gong around the market with details of the missing child; this systems works so effectively, no mother is ever worried about where her child might be at any time, since all mothers know their children are safe.

6. Ensuring that the market place is clean, that no rubbish or dangerous implements are left lying around.

7. Investigating any strange faces and their intentions in the market

Igueben Market: traders rise early to be allocated a good stall

In the ancient kingdom, the Ikeki was supported by a team of staff including messengers, helpers, criers and runners who helped him with these tasks. Without the Ikeki, the Edo markets would not have been so efficiently and effectively ran.

A modern Ikeki has access to mobile phones and loudspeakers to help with communication. He does not use runners anymore; his helpers and messengers use modern vehicles like motorcycles or bicycles to deliver messages.

What people do at the market?

Mostly the market place is used as a forum for sharing information e.g. a new birth in the family, on this occasion the lucky family rub the upper part of their bodies with dusting powder and wear tiny coral beads, this dress code signifies announcement of a new arrival in the family.

Informal disputes can be settled as the offended and the offender come face to face before an impartial audience who will listen to both sides and offer advice on how both parties should proceed. With many people around to hear the case, the dispute is resolved with apologises and remedies accepted and the case is settled; in the case that this is not resolved, the matter will be taken to the palace, where the council of chiefs can listen to both sides; establish the facts and deliberate on the issues; they decide the merits of both sides accounts and their decision is final.

People buy and sell things or simply exchange them.

Food items are also sold or exchanged; these being excess food people have left over after storing what they need away, they happily exchange these for other commodities or food items they are short of. Edo people are good and industrious farmers.

Children use the opportunity to meet up with their friends; sometimes completing some mischief they had embarked on earlier.

Women use the opportunity to share gossips e.g. 'Did you know that that one's wife ran back home to her parents after an argument with the senior wife?' etc.

Items sold and exchanged in the market include, fabric, meats, fish, herbs, vegetables, fruit, household hold utensil, baskets and including all other manner of items.

Imported goods and items that are not available in Benin are also bought and exchanged e.g. rice, salt, certain fabric, etc.

The market square is the place to be on market days, elderly and sick people who cannot get there eagerly await the moment others return with presents for them and to share latest gossip or news including political developments.

Market days provide Edo people opportunities to practice and keep another aspect of their rich culture alive.

Market women proudly show visitors around their market

# Illness and Health

The Edo had intimate knowledge of the rainforest. They believed that leaves and herbs had divine powers to preserve life through the god Osun, their god of the rainforest. They therefore treated the rainforest with reverence taking from it only that which they needed.

Edo doctors and herbalist knew which trees and herbs were effective for different conditions. They had good knowledge of which ones produced hallucinations and other euphoric conditions. They were able to combine different leaves, tree backs and herbs to cure people of most illness or achieve effects like hallucination. This knowledge and skills gave some of them mystical status.

The palace had a team of doctors and herbalists who looked after the health of the king's wives and children. Their knowledge of the medicinal properties of forest trees was phenomena; knowledge which they preserved and passed down over generations.

The method of treating malaria by simmering different medicinal leaves, tree barks and herbs from the forest is still used effectively today.

Here is an extract of a diary entry made by a sick child in 1997: *'Mum lifted me gently onto the chair, in front of which a big cauldron was steaming with all sorts of medicinal smells. Mum put a blanket over my head and the cauldron, asking me to take a deep breath. This was repeated about six times until I broke out in a sweat. 'Good;' she said, 'all the toxins are coming out with the sweat.' She then took me outside and bathed me with some of the concoction, she explained that the toxins needed to be acted on from all fronts: through my airways, hence the breathing in of the steam from the cauldron exercise; through the skin pores (osmosis during the bathing) and through my digestive system - my mouth and stomach. After my bath, mum gave me a warm cupful of the concoction. She did try to make me eat something but all I wanted to do was sleep, so she put me back in bed.'*

This child was well again within five days, back to good health.

Food and health

The rainforest also provided a wide variety of vegetables and fruit that contributed to Edo people's good health.

Mangoes

Sweet potatoes

Grapefruit

Below are some Edo recipes that ensured good health.

# Edo recipes

## Fried Plantains

INGREDIENTS:
Serves 4
1/2 Cup cooking oil
3 plantains
1 small onion

1. Slice the plantain into rounds or oblong, about 1cm thick
2. Heat the oil in a large frying pan over medium heat.
3. Very carefully, fry the pieces till the edges are very lightly golden brown.
4. Turn them over, and fry the other side until golden brown.
5. Chop the onion and brown lightly
6. Drain excess oil with a paper towel.
7. Serve immediately with the fried onion and seasoned vegetables

Perfect with a choice from:
Egg and corned beef omelette.
Spinach sauce with tomato
Tomato ketchup
Fried fish with sweet peppers

Hot Tip: Ripe plantain also taste good roasted, boiled or baked.

# Mai-Mai

## INGREDIENTS

Serves 4

1 cup bean powder
1 small onion
1 red chili peppers
1 red sweet pepper
1/2 cup diced cooked chicken (optional)
1 cup chicken stock
salt and pepper
4 small-sized tin foil containers

## Method

1. Blend onion and peppers together
2. Place the bean powder in a large bowl and use the chicken sauce to make a smooth paste of medium consistency
3. Mix in the blended onion and peppers and diced chicken
4. Add salt and pepper to taste
5. Spoon into tin foil containers. Fill up to about 3/4, full as mixture rises during cooking.
6. Bring some water to boil in a steaming sauce pan.
7. Arrange the tin foil container in the pan and cover.
8. Steam for 40 - 45 minutes.
9. Serve hot or cold with fried rice, jollof rice, plantain or white rice and seasoned vegetables.


Tips: Also taste good when cooked with boiled fish or egg, corned beef and other meat products instead of chicken. Garnish with vegetables and tomato sauce.

Jollof Rice with chicken

## INGREDIENTS

Serves 4
**2 cups long grain rice**
*1 tbsp cooking oil*
*1 medium onion, finely chopped*
*2 red chilli peppers*
*6 fresh tomatoes or 400g peeled chopped tomatoes*
*2tbsp tomato puree*
**Chicken stock**
*Salt*
1 small chicken, cut into small pieces

## Method

1. Parboil the chicken and deep fry in hot oil. Season and put into a warm oven to keep warm
2. Make the tomato sauce by blending together the chilli pepper and tomatoes
3. Heat 1tbsp of oil in a frying pan and gently brown the onion, add the blended tomato and puree and cook until tender.
4. Boil the rice until tender and soft.
5. When all the water has evaporated, add the tomato sauce.
6. Simmer in very low heat for 2 to 3 minutes for rice to absorb tomato flavour.
7. Serve immediately with prepared fried chicken.

Hot tip: Side dish can include fried plantain, boiled beans, vegetables and salads.

# Oral stories

The Edos have a great oral tradition through which they use stories and proverbs to teach the young generation about their history and moral issues. A Benin storyteller is a learned entertainer and historian in one. The village elders memorize the genealogy, or family or village history going back centuries. Through Bini stories we can also learn a great deal about their way of life.

The first story relates a way in which someone could become a slave in those days. It sheds light into reasons why Edo did not maltreat their slaves as others did, knowing that anyone could fall on hard times. Edo treated other people as they would want to be treated. This was one of their golden principles.

Bose's Despair

Bose's family need money very quickly to buy herbs for their sick first born son, if he does not receive any treatment, he will die from his fever.

They approach Mama Omon, the local women's group leader. She lends them money on the understanding that they will pay back by next full moon plus 2(three months). Three months go by and Bose's baby brother is well again but the family have fallen on hard times and cannot pay back what they owe Mama Omon.

After repeated demands to no avail, in fact one full moon plus five has gone by (six months) and it seems Mama Omon is never going to get back her money . She takes the case to the Enogie (the local chief).

After both sides present their cases, the Enogie deliberates with his chiefs, it is decided that Bose is to be given in payment to Mama Omon, she is to work out a term that equals the amount owed and then sent back home to her family unless Bose's parents borrow more money from Mama Omon; in which case Bose must remain with Mama Omon to work out the value of this amount.

Bose immediately goes with Mama Omon, from now on she is to be known as Mama Omon's slave, worse still, if fortunes do not change for her parents and they fail to pay back money owed to Mama Omon. She could remain a slave for the rest of her life.

Bose is now a slave girl.

## **The Tortoise and The Dog**

Once upon a time, the dog and the tortoise got involved in a challenge to see which of them ran the fastest.

The dog said it would run faster than the tortoise, while the tortoise said no it would run faster. The dog laughed at the tortoise saying that the tortoise moves slow and indeed was the slowest moving animal in the animal kingdom.

They then set a day to prove once and for all, which of them ran fastest.

Even though the tortoise was the slowest moving in the animal kingdom, it was regarded as the smartest.

Prior to the day of the race, the tortoise enlisted the help of some other tortoises. The other tortoises were strategically placed along the route so that the dog would think he was seeing the same tortoise in the race with him.

At each point, the dog saw a tortoise and wondered how the tortoise had over-run him. The dog ran faster. Then on the next location, he saw another tortoise but the dog thought he was seeing the same tortoise in the race with him.

At the final stop, the dog arrived panting and out of breath, yet there was the tortoise looking fresh and relaxed. The dog wondered how this could have happened since naturally the tortoise walked slower than other animals.

Of course he did not know that he had run the race with many tortoises.

The Tortoise won the prize.

### **Jealousy does not pay**

Once upon a time, there lived in a village a man who had two wives. The first and older wife had only one daughter whom she named Omokherebhe (meaning a child is more important than anything else). This girl was the most beautiful girl in the whole village. Every other girl wanted her to be their friend but her mother named Odion was very protective of her and would not allow her out. Though she had friends, they could only come to her home to visit her. She was never allowed to go out to visit them; for fear that she might come to some harm.

The second wife Ukele, also had a daughter and other children. The girl's name was Anonhen. She was a very deceitful girl and full of envy and jealousy. She was not very beautiful and wished that she was as beautiful as Omokherebhe.

To keep Omokherebhe busy when she was out, her mother would ask her to sweep, clean and cook. The mother would put a stone in a cooking pot and tell her to cook it until it was nice and tender. Omokherebhe would cook and cook the stone, but it was never done. When the mother arrived home, she would commend her for a job well done and reward her with every good thing to make her look more beautiful. Whenever her friends came and asked her to go out some place to play, Omokherebhe would tell them that she was busy.

One day, Anonhen the step sister came and asked her to go out with her and some friends. Again, Omokherebhe refused giving the same excuse that she was busy. Anonhen went to the backyard, got some green leaves and secretly placed them over the stone. Herself and the rest of the girls helped Omokherebhe to complete her chores. Then Anonhen went to the pot, touched the leaves with a knife and shouted that the stone was cooked!!!

All the girls then went to the forest to gather fire wood. While they were out, Anonhen convinced Omokherebhe to climb up a tree and cut down one of the branches. When Omokherebhe was up on the tree, Anonhen set it on fire. Omokherebhe was burnt to ashes. The ashes were white and beautiful just like she was in real life. The girls went home and said nothing.

When Odion her mother arrived home from the market, her daughter was gone. She searched everywhere and asked all the girls. They denied knowing anything. At first she was angry that her daughter had disobeyed her orders. But when she looked into the cooking pot and found the leaves, she knew that her daughter had been deceived into going out.

Odion and her husband went to the village Wise One to find out what had happened. The Wise One told them that her daughter was dead, burnt alive. He told them to go and collect all the ashes and bring them to him. They did.

The Wise One told them that he was going to cook the ashes for seven days and if Omokherebhe killed herself, the ashes would turn to worms but if she had been killed by anyone else, then she would be brought back to life looking more beautiful than ever.. As soon as Anonhen heard that, she too wanted to be re-incarnated. She pestered her equally jealous mother until they hatched a plan to secretly burn Anonhen so her ashes could be brought to the Wise One.

Anonhen and her mother went out together. The mother set fire to the tree after Anonhen had climbed up one of the branches. The tree and Anohen produced dark and ugly ashes. The mother went crying into the village that her daughter was missing. She and the father went to the Wise One who told them to do exactly as was done in Omokherebhe's situation. The ashes were gathered and placed in another pot.

The Wise One cooked both pots for seven days. On the seventh day, there was pomp and pageantry as both mothers went to see the Wise One.

When they arrived there, the Wise One repeated what had happened and why they were there. He told them that the daughter who was truly murdered would re-appear looking more beautiful than ever, while the one who caused her own death would turn into worms. With the whole village looking, the Wise One first opened Omokherebhe's pot. Out walked Omokherebhe looking like an angel, more beautiful than ever. The whole village gasped at her radiance and applauded.

Then it was time to open the other pot. The Wise One walked up to the pot and opened it. Inside of the pot were worms, worms and more worms. Again, the whole village gasped.

Anonhen had turned into worms. Her mother went home weeping while Omokherebhe and her mother went home rejoicing.

Anonhen's mother had to pay for a cleansing ceremony to rid the village of worms.

### Activities:
A Bini creation story: Illustrate each section of the story.
Combine your illustrations as a single cartoon strip.

Bose's Despair: This story has no dialogue. Rewrite adding dialogue.

The Tortoise and the Dog: Write a playscript for this story. Present to other classes or in whole school assembly.

# Activities and games

## Children's games

### Last leg game

A game for any number of children

What to do:

Choose a counter; all others sit in a circle around the counter. Everyone to stretch their legs out in front of them so the counter can touch each. When the counter starts singing, the game begins and she touches each person's foot until the last word in the song. That leg is eliminated from the game. Owner of leg tucks it back behind them. The game continues until only one leg is left. The owner of that leg is the winner (like musical chairs).

### Song/ nonsense rhyme

Gbolo
Gbeva
Tise
Teghele
Tebule
Nopka
Nusen
Nogolo
Node
Ya!

Activity idea: Try writing your own nonsense rhymes in English for this game.

### The okoki game

A game for any number of children

How to play:

Everyone sits in a big wide circle, legs crossed. A catcher is selected and given a parcel (bean bag, box, anything will do).

Everyone must look up straight ahead of them so they cannot see what the catcher is doing behind when they go past them. Cheating means exclusion from this and other games for the night. In a phrase and response song (below), the catcher walks gently round the back of the circle and during this time must drop their object behind one of the players who will not notice, the catcher goes all the way round the circle and she gets to the target, she taps her on the back to indicate that she has got to chase. The catcher runs round the circle as fast as she can to take up the space vacated by the target. If she succeeds the target becomes the catcher otherwise the game continues. The target must start to chase as soon she is aware of the object behind her.

**Song:**

**Phrase: Okoki izaghin eheen**

**Response: izaghin**

**Phrase: Okoki izaghin eheen**

**Response: izaghin**

**Phrase: Okoki izaghin eheen**

**Response: izaghin**

**Phrase: Okoki izaghin eheen**

**Response: izaghin**

Tempo increases as game / chase increases.

## The River song

Eriuoko riesse o-o –o, esse reioroke, abuwon waagbon o- o- o, ehie go ho ma kchia le.

(*I took my calabash to the river, the river has taken it upstream, the happenings of this world are predestined*).

Activity idea:
**Learn this simple song, make lyrics for it and accompany with dance moves. Present to your school assembly.**

## Ayo game

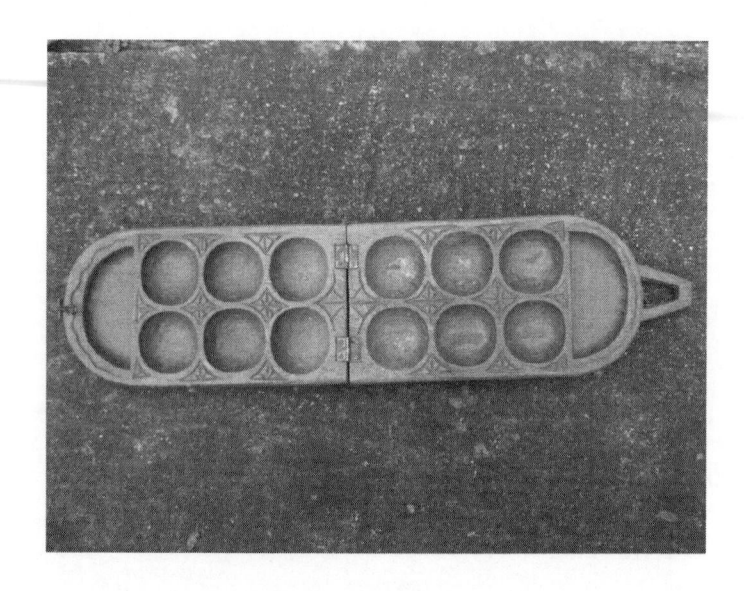

## A game for 2-4 players

<u>You will need: 48 counters</u>

2 players 24 counters each with 6 counter ridges

3 players 16 counters each with 4 counter ridges.

4 players 12 counters each with 3 counter ridges.

***Aim of the game*** is to win all your opponents counters and make them bankrupt. They are out of the game when they have lost all their counters. Everyone starts with four counters in each ridge. Simple counting game, player A starts by collecting all 4 counters from a ridge, counts on and collects all the counters in the last stop, they carry on until they run out of counters or they make a complete house of four. They keep this as their winning in their bank. The game ends when a player has taken all the counters off their opponent.

Activity idea:
**Challenge see if you can design your own version of this game.**

Quiz

## The Great Kingdom of Benin quizzes.

1. The Great kingdom of Benin was destroyed in

    a) 1066, b) 1897 c) 1914

2. The first kings to rule Benin were

a) Eweka b) Oranmiyan c) Ogisos

3. Benin is located on a rolling coastal plain of a

a) The Middle East b) Iceland c) Tropical Rainforest

4. The First Europeans to visit the Kingdom of Benin were:

a) The Portuguese b) the Spanish c) the British

5. The Benin call themselves, their language and their land:

a) The Yorubas b) The Ishekiris c) The Edos

6. Ancient Benin Kingdom traded in:

a) Brass, ivory and textiles, b) gold c) slaves.

7. The rightful heir to the throne is:

a) the first born daughter, b) the last born son c) the first born son

8. The Benin warrior kings reigned around:

a) the 15th century b) the 13th century c) the 17th century

9. The major currency used in trade by the Edo people was the:

a) the naira b) the Kobo c) cowrie shells

10. The Edo patron god of metal is:

a) Ogun, b) Osun, c)Olokun

11. The Edo patron god of the rainforest, leaves and herbs is:

a) Ogun, b) Osun, c)Olokun

12. The British Punitive raid took place between:

a) January & February 1897 b) January & February 1879

b) c) January & February 1697

13. The Oba could not receive the British Envoy because:

a) he could not be bothered b) he was on holiday c) he was engaged in important ancestral rituals

14. The raid last:

a) one day b) two years c) two months

15. During the raid the Oba was:

a) killed b) sent into exile on a boat c) restored to power

16. During the raid, all the royalties and chiefs were:

a) killed b) sent into exile on a boat c) restored to power.

17. With the Oba gone, the Edo people:

a) celebrated b) fled c) continued to fight

18. The Modern Royal dynasty was restored in:

A, 1897 b) 1940 c) 1914

19. The forgers of the iron ceremonial swords (*eben*) were from:

a) Oka b) Igueben, c) Benin city

20. The Edo people are very proud of:

a) their past achievements b) the capital city c) the people

**Answers:**

1. **b**
2. **c**
3. **c**
4. **a**
5. **c**
6. **a**
7. **c**
8. **a**
9. **c**
10. **a**
11. **b**
12. **a**
13. **c**
14. **c**
15. **b**
16. **a**
17. **b**
18. **c**
19. **b**
20. **a**

# Word puzzles

## The Great Kingdom of Benin word puzzles

| G | C | d | j | v | o | r | a | n | m | i | y | a | n | P | e | p | a | g | e |
|---|---|---|---|---|---|---|---|---|---|---|---|---|---|---|---|---|---|---|---|
| L | E | a | r | b | l | n | c | t | d | k | d | d | w | T | x | m | G | g | h |
| C | R | r | g | s | O | l | z | w | o | p | r | a | f | W | N | j | B | v | e |
| G | E | b | e | n | K | d | j | b | t | y | f | h | s | C | I | h | O | v | i |
| P | M | d | f | n | U | u | r | b | f | a | l | b | h | A | N | d | N | a | p |
| X | O | d | z | u | n | h | q | w | y | g | a | s | k | N | E | v | d | x | s |
| D | N | p | f | d | r | k | n | c | z | a | y | q | s | D | B | g | a | d | v |
| L | Y | f | s | a | e | r | g | o | b | a | f | g | y | T | h | v | s | b | L |
| V | s | g | j | w | s | h | j | r | e | h | t | o | m | N | e | e | u | q | F |
| O | d | e | n | m | f | s | a | d | a | b | k | o | p | G | s | a | d | f | e |
| D | f | a | a | l | c | o | r | a | l | b | e | a | d | S | g | s | x | z | R |
| J | o | e | w | z | q | t | r | e | f | h | n | v | x | C | B | k | n | a | z |
| D | f | z | e | s | e | d | a | r | e | u | q | s | a | M | d | o | a | d | c |
| E | d | k | u | c | i | r | t | s | v | W | g | s | e | Q | r | f | d | h | x |
| A | d | b | x | v | m | n | v | x | w | E | g | u | p | B | j | f | i | s | v |
| D | b | i | t | y | f | i | b | k | i | A | j | g | t | V | x | e | a | o | i |
| F | v | b | u | g | h | k | r | z | a | V | e | w | r | T | f | g | l | p | y |
| A | s | q | r | t | f | v | s | p | d | E | f | v | n | S | f | d | f | k | h |
| U | t | s | s | a | f | s | d | f | s | R | e | y | t | I | u | y | d | e | c |
| C | a | s | s | a | v | a | a | d | e | s | v | m | j | I | o | g | i | s | o |

**Oranmiyan, Ogiso, cassava, Oba, agbon, eben, ada, Olokun, chiefs, Benin, Edo, ceremony, bronzes, coral, beads, trade, weavers, masquerade, page, prince, queen mother.**

Solution is on the next page.

# Solution

**The Great Kingdom of Benin word puzzles solution**

|   | C |   |   |   | o | r | a | n | m | i | y | a | n |   | p | a | g | e |
|---|---|---|---|---|---|---|---|---|---|---|---|---|---|---|---|---|---|---|
|   | E |   |   |   | l |   |   |   |   | d |   |   |   |   | G |   |   |   |
|   | R |   |   |   | O |   |   |   |   |   | a |   |   | N |   | B |   |   |
|   | E | b | e | n | K |   |   |   |   |   |   |   |   | I |   | O |   |   |
|   | M |   |   |   | U |   |   |   |   |   |   |   |   | N |   | N |   |   |
|   | O |   |   |   | n |   |   |   |   |   |   |   |   | E |   |   |   |   |
|   | N |   |   |   |   |   |   |   |   |   |   |   |   | B |   |   |   |   |
|   | Y |   |   |   |   |   |   | o | b | a |   |   |   |   |   |   |   |   |
|   |   |   |   |   |   |   | r | e | h | t | o | m | N | e | e | u | q |   |
| o | d | e |   |   |   |   |   |   |   |   |   |   |   |   |   |   |   | e |
|   |   |   |   |   | c | o | r | a | l | b | e | a | d | S |   |   | z |   |
|   |   |   |   |   |   |   |   |   |   |   |   |   |   |   |   | n |   |   |
|   |   |   | e |   | e | d | a | r | e | u | q | s | a | M |   | o |   | c |
| e |   |   | c |   |   |   |   |   | W |   |   |   |   | r |   |   | h |   |
|   | d |   |   |   | n |   |   |   | E |   |   |   | B |   |   | i |   |   |
|   |   | a |   |   |   | i |   |   | A |   |   |   |   | e |   |   |   |   |
|   |   | r |   |   |   | r |   |   | V |   |   |   | f |   |   |   |   |   |
|   |   |   | t |   |   |   | p |   | E |   |   | S |   |   |   |   |   |   |
|   |   |   |   |   |   |   |   |   | R |   |   |   |   |   |   |   |   |   |
| c | a | s | s | a | v | a |   |   | s |   |   |   |   | o | g | i | s | o |

**Oranmiyan Ogiso cassava Oba agbon eben ada Olokun chiefs Benin Edo ceremony bronzes coral beads trade weavers masquerade page, prince queen mother**

# Glossary

## Benin Background page

Ancient - a long time ago

Chieftaincy - high ranking official

Customs - people's way of life

Divine - being or having the nature of a god

Forest Kingdom - a forest area that were ruled by a local king

Heir - successor: a person who inherits some title or office

Oral traditions - passed down from generation to generation by word of mouth.

Shrine - An altar or niche dedicated to a particular Goddess or God and held to be sacred.

Virtue - the quality of doing what is right and avoiding what is wrong.


## Edo Calendar and seasons

Lunar – this calendar system uses phases of the moon.

Solar year – is the amount of time it takes the sun return to the same position in the cycle of seasons.

Lunisolar – a calendar system used by many cultures which combine the lunar and solar systems. It indicates the season and phases of the moon.

## Childhood page

Commerce - trade or exchange of goods and money.

Crop preservation - the activity of protecting the yield from plants in a single growing season from loss or danger

Drought - a prolonged period of dryness that can cause damage to plants.

Games - animals hunted for food or sport.

Produce - fresh fruits and vegetable grown for the market.

## Trade and Commerce page

Blacksmith - A crafter of iron and steel.

Coral beads - Beads made from the hard stony skeleton of a Mediterranean coral that has a delicate red or pink colour

Cowrie shells - marine snails of the genus Cypraea (family Cypraeidae), found chiefly in tropical regions, especially around the Maldives or the East Indies. The shell itself is smooth and more or less egg-shaped, with a long, narrow, slit-like opening (aperture).

Dialects - a particular version of a language with its own distinctive accent, grammar and vocabulary.

Rural - sparsely settled places away from the influence of large cities and towns

Suitor - a man who courts a woman

# Further reading

Web links:

http://www.bbc.co.uk/schools/primaryhistory/worldhistory/benin_bronze/

http://beninhistorya.blogspot.co.uk/

http://iyiomon.blogspot.co.uk/

http://www.britishmuseum.org/PDF/british_museum_benin_art.pdf

http://www.conceptvessel.net/iyare/index.html

http://edoworld.net/Benin_bronze.html

http://www.edoworld.net/Edo_people.html

http://edoworld.net/Obas.html

http://en.wikipedia.org/wiki/Benin_Empire#Monarchs

http://en.wikipedia.org/wiki/Oba_of_Benin

# Inside A Rainforest Royal Court

## Historical enquiry

*Fidelia Nimmons*

# Contents

| | |
|---|---|
| Preface | 113 |
| Pupils activities | 116 |
| Burial ceremonies | 118 |
| Artwork | 120 |
| Genealogy | 124 |
| Food production | 126 |
| Extended Family system | 127 |
| Wedding ceremonies | 128 |
| Dress and fashion | 130 |
| Stories and Myths | 131 |
| Other activities | 132 |
| Medieval Kingdoms: A comparison | 134 |
| Activities on the whole book | 139 |
| Review of historical enquiry unit | 145 |

# Kingdom of Benin Activities
# Historical enquiry

Preface

This section of the book contain activities which will engage pupils in carrying out full historical enquiries into the Kingdom of Benin and provide lots of fun things to do along the way.

Activities will involve pupils in researching information in books and on the internet.

Resources needed include:

1. Internet access
2. Writing material e.g. pencil and paper.
3. Art equipment e.g. clay and drawing materials
4. Blank world map

*Children will learn how to:*

- Carry out an historical enquiry.
- Identify a variety of sources of information using primary and secondary sources- oral history, artefacts, historical accounts from the past, photographs.
- Distinguish between relevant and irrelevant information and events placing ideas in order, chronological and other.
- Differentiate fact from opinion.
- Increase their knowledge of Black and African history.
- Synthesize information gathered from study and research.

## Sources of historical evidence:

There are two sources of historical evidence, primary and secondary.

Primary evidence is a firsthand account of an event and includes diaries, journals, letters, speeches, news stories, photographs, and pieces of art:

Secondary evidence sources are works that are based on analysis of primary sources, such as textbooks, biographies, nonfiction books about history and monographs; they often also include quotations or illustrations from primary sources.

Oral traditions and oral histories are as old as humanity and provide another way to learn about the past from people with firsthand knowledge of historical events. Most African history is passed down this way as tribal and community leaders and other witnesses pass information from generation to generation using stories, anecdotes, songs and their daily practice of their customs.

This material meets the two historical sources rules:

**Time and place rule**: Events referred to are documented as they happen and the author is a direct participant at the events and if not; interviewed those involved immediately afterwards for example interment of a late Edo Chief procedures.

**The bias rule:** all of the evidence has been cross checked with other sources and related evidence e.g. celebrations and ceremonies by the Edo Royal Court have been crossed checked against bronze plaques made 400 – 500 years ago. Engravings by the Dutch artist Dapper of 1668 is compared with modern day practices of Edo Royal processions and plaque records. Edo's own record of their history through various art works have been analysed and checked against written records by European traders from the 14the century onwards and including British troops records in 1897.

## **Vocabulary**

Historical source
Primary source
Secondary source
Oral history
Written history
Evidence
Genealogy
Beliefs
Customs
Myths
Traditions
King
Kingdom
Oba
chief
Artwork
Mosaic
Frescoes
Necropolis
Fallow
Immortality
Monastery
Patron Saint
Venerate
Shroud / Mat shroud
Casket
Soldiers
Warriors
Plaque
Terracotta
Edo people
Benin people
Bini people
The Edos
The Binis

# Pupils' activities:
## Considering evidence
## Royal court ceremonies

Oba of Benin, Igue procession, Dapper 1668. Notice the singers and dancers surrounding him, and the long procession of people.

Chief Ebenzer of Igueben conferment walkabout 1996, notice the procession of people, musicians in the background. Compare this picture to the one above

FN in an Eben dance procession at Chief Ebenezer's burial ceremony 2007

## Questions on the pictures

What can you see happening in each picture?

What are the same about all three pictures?

What are the differences between the pictures?

What do these pictures tell us about the Edo way of life?

## General questions:

From the pictures, what would you say have changed since 1668 and present day?

What has remained the same?

What do we learn about Edo history from the pictures and videos?

### Burial ceremonies

Just like the Ancient Egyptians, Greeks, and Romans, the Ancient Edo people believed in the afterlife; and burial of the dead included providing them with what they would need to carry on their lives in the afterlife, including burying kings with a host of servants and maids together with items for daily survival e.g. food.

The ancient Egyptians had a tradition that tombs where nobles were buried should resemble the houses of the living, as the tomb was the house of the dead. This tradition influenced both the Greeks and Romans burial practices. The Edo also held similar beliefs. Whilst evidence for this tradition for the other civilisations lie in the archaeological finds and well preserved structures they left behind, the Edo continue to retain aspects of this tradition in burying their nobles in houses where they can remain in the comfort of their own homes and where their burial place can be easy identified; so their stories are not forgotten.

### Look at these pictures:

Tombs of the kings, excavated in 1977, in Pafos, Cyprus, caved into solid rocks, they derived from Egyptian tradition and feature Greek architecture. Used for burying nobles, they date back to 300BC and 300AD and were plastered and covered with frescoes. The nobles were buried with personal items and belongings.

Burial place of Prince Omhelimhen Okunsebor in 2006. This was his home, where he was buried in his bedroom. The house is part of a larger compound with modern houses for his family. Notice the people standing in front of the house, they keep his room locked and clean. As per tradition, this house as much as possible must be preserved for eternity and as the burial place of the prince, must be revered and respected. The Prince is never to be disturbed.

In the absence of solid rocks to chisel into in the rainforests, the Edo use this method to protect their dead for eternity.

Questions:

What are the similarities between the two pictures above?

What are the differences?

Name the similarities between the burial traditions.

Edo still bury their nobles in their own homes, what do you think has made it possible for the them to carry on with this tradition?

Which other aspects of ancient burial traditions do you think would be sensible for the Edo people to retain? Why do you think so?

## **Artwork**

Throughout history and across cultures, people have recorded their own story through their art work.

Edo brass work showing the Oba and the Queen Mother with dancers and drummers. We can tell how the Oba and Queens dressed, how the dancers and drummers dressed and what instruments they used for music making. These practices were recorded in their bronze plaques over 500 hundred years ago and the practice still exists today.

The Oba wears beaded crown and royal regalia, carrying the Eben, his staff of authority.

The dancer is fully adorned with beads on the ankles, wrist, waist, neck, and head. She holds a hand fan for cooling herself whilst dancing.

The drummer balances his drum between his knees to get the right beat.

Edo wood carving: showing a woman carrying calabash gourd on her head; probably containing farm crops. We can tell female hair styles, means of transporting objects and equipment used at the time from this wood carving.

Analysing scenes shown on various brass work, wood carvings and terracotta sculptures provide strong evidence for deducing about how the people lived, what jobs they did and pastimes they engaged in. These are strong historical evidence to support our study of the great kingdom..

Holy Kykkos Monastery Cyprus frescoes; showing the crucifixion of St Paul. The Christians used mosaic and frescoes to depict bible stories and significant events in their history.

Statue of the Goddess Aphrodite, the Greeks used marble statues to record their religious beliefs and significant events in their history e.g. The first Olympic games.

Dating back to 3rd AD: Roman mosaic floor in The House of Aion, Kato Pafos, showing the myth Apollo and Marysos. Roman houses used spectacular mosaics to depict scenes from ancient Greek mythologies and to show their wealth. The Roman emperors used columns to depict their wealth, power and accomplishments. The Benin kings used bronze plaques for the same purposes.

## Questions

Why do you think different cultures across times and places have used artwork to record their history?

What methods are used to record historical events today?

## Genealogy:

With written records, family trees help us record our relatives and ancestors lineage and to trace our ancestry. Edos do this effectively by naming their new born babies after significant relatives of the past. They are able to pass on stories of significant events and achievements, this way; they are also able to date events accurately using this method. Through this child naming system, stories of events up to the fourth and fifth generation and beyond are accurately retold and passed on. This places notable sons and daughters and significant events firmly in their oral history.

Here is a simple Edo family genealogy:

Baby boy born in July 2009 named: Omeike

| | |
|---|---|
| He is first son of | Ozin |
| Who is son of | Odigie |
| Who is son of | Aigbogun |
| Who is son of | Omeike (DOB: late 1800s and a famous blacksmith) |

**Look at this picture**

This Christian church, like others has used icons and paintings to record significant persons in the church's history in chronological order. This serves the same purpose as a family tree or genealogy in helping trace significant people in their history.

**Questions**
What are the similarities between the Benin genealogy system and the Church's? What are the differences between both systems?

Research and draw your family tree. What does it look like?

## Food production:

### Land fallow and crop rotation

Look at this picture

A piece of land is left fallow and will be farmed next year. This method along with crop rotation, improve soil fertility naturally. We know how Edo cultivated their lands successfully from some of their bronze plaque records and from their current practices.

### Questions:

What can you see in the picture above?

Who do think owns this land?

What can you see in the background?

Why has the land been left fallow?

What methods are used today to improve soil fertility and crop yield?

Which soil improvement methods, would you say is most environmentally friendly and why?

## **Extended family system:**

Questions:

Who are these people?

What are they doing?

Why are there so many members in one family?

What do you think the occasion was for this photograph was?
Give your evidence.

What are the advantages of belonging to an extended family? What are the disadvantages?

With the advancement of technology – Skype, face book, webcams, emails, twitters and the internet, what advantages and challenges do you think these family members face when communicating with each other; or with the whole group?

Would you like to belong to an extended family like this? Why?

## **Wedding Ceremonies**

No wedding is considered binding in Edo culture without the native traditional wedding; which provide more opportunities to sing, dance and celebrate. A dowry price must be negotiated and paid by the groom's family to compensate the bride's family for the loss of her labour and earnings powers.

Look at these pictures:

Identity parade; which is your bride? The groom must identify his bride from a number of covered up maidens or be sent packing as not truly knowing his bride to be.

The bride's father has to formally bless her before giving her away.

**Questions:**

Look at the first picture; what jobs do you think the girls in the picture do? How do you know?

Look at the second picture. What job do you think the bride's father does? How do you know?

The bride is a lawyer, how much dowry do you think the groom was levelled this time?

(Answer for question 1 above in order- hospital matron, trainee doctor, pharmacist; question 2 – a barrister)

## **Dress and fashion**

Look at this picture

Questions:

Explain what you can see happening in this photograph.

Who are these people?

Where are they going or coming from? (Answer: church service)

Can you identify their fashion style?

Imagine a conversation between two of the people, what will they say to each other? Draw speech bubbles to show this.

Freeze frame part of the photograph and dramatise what is happening, what happened before now? What happened afterwards?

Now unfreeze the scene for some thought tapping. Choose three or four characters. Each character on cue (tap on the shoulder), completes this sentence: 'I am looking forward to ....'

You are one of the people in the picture; make an entry on your twitter web page about the church service. Remember you must not use more than 140 characters including spacing between words.

Pick one of the outfits to make a drawing of.

**Stories and Myths**

Just like other cultures, Edo tell the mythical story of how Osanobua the high King of the sky first created the world, he is still considered the utterly benevolent and universal God Osanubua. The first kings of Benin, the Ogiso kings are said to have descended from him and they appealed to him as a last resort when all else had failed. This was the same belief held by the Ancient Greeks and Romans and which form the basis of the creation story in book of Genesis in the bible.

Read the full story in volume 1 of this book. Find a copy of the bible and compare Benin creation story with that in the book of Genesis. What similarities and differences can you find?

**Look at this picture**

St George is the patron Saint of a lot of countries, including England, Russia and Greece. He is also patron saint of cities like Gozo, Moscow, etc and of lots of organizations e.g. Scouts, professions e.g. the military and of some disease sufferers e.g. skin disease. Even though, the story of St. George and the Dragon is a myth, he continues to be venerated across the world.

**Questions**

Research the story of St George and the Dragon, summarise the story in your own words.

Read the statement below and say where it was always true, sometimes true or never true. Give evidence to support your stand.

*'In the absence of science, different cultures in the past relied on mythical stories to explain natural phenomenon.'*

**Other activities**

Research and produce a timeline of the Kings of Benin.

Watch the Igu'Oba video; make a sketch of two chiefs, one in red and one in white, find out the significance of these colours for the Edo people.
*http://www.youtube.com/watch?v=okn1nwnCQBQ&feature=related*

Watch the Edo chiefs dancing in the video, why do you think there are no females? How do you think the females would be feeling watching only men dancing in the celebration of their cultural ceremonies, what makes you say that?

Research the significance of red and white colours in Edo customs.

It is Edo custom that the Oba never leaves the palace, except during the Igue festival as depicted in Dapper's engraving of 1668 and shown in the Igie ErhOba video. Compare the video with the engraving; do you think Dapper's engraving was an accurate representation of this festival? What is your evidence for this view?

Research Kingdom of Benin 15th & 16th century trade with the Europeans? Produce a guide booklet on 'Trading with The Kingdom of Benin'

You are an Edo chief; write a blog about your dance for the king on your web page. How did you feel a day before, on the morning of the day? What do you think of the other chiefs? Did any of them get on your nerves or try to out-dance you? Did the Oba say anything to you? How did you feel during your dance? How did you feel at the end of the dance?

Imagine you are one of the spectators at the Igu'Oba festival; send a post card home to England about your experiences.

If you had an Edo heritage, which customs would you observe and which would you not; and why?

Produce an illustrated booklet for *The Great Kingdom of Benin*.

### **Weighing it up**

As a class, debate the topic 'Not all historical evidence holds equal value'

Rank the following historical evidence in order of reliability giving your reasons.

**diaries, journals, letters, speeches, news stories, photographs, and pieces of art, paintings, films, textbooks, biographies, popular songs, stock inventories, oral stories, stories and tales, museum artefacts, genealogy, interviews, customs and way of life.**

## Medieval Kingdoms
## A comparison between the English and the Benin Medieval Kingdoms

We know from evidence that during the medieval period - the period after the last Roman emperor was disposed (A.D. 476) and the Italian Renaissance period (A.D.1453) people across the world did things in similar ways right up the 16th century.

We know further that the Kingdom of Benin was at its height at the same time as European Renaissance was (14th to 16th centuries). We know this from records including oral and written accounts and various forms of art including paintings and the Benin bronzes.

We can delve back to this period in world history to examine living conditions for the kings. We can compare court life in Europe and Kingdom of Benin. As it was Britain that sacked Benin, it is prudent to make the comparison between these two Kingdoms.

**Activity 1**

**Historical enquiry: Imagine that you travelled back in time to this period (A.D. 476 – 1453), use the information below to help you write an illustrated booklet on *Medieval Kingdoms*.**

### Religious Beliefs

Peoples of both kingdoms held mythical beliefs e.g. believing in the power of the supreme god to punish or reward according to their deeds. Source: Church's religious beliefs.

### The kings

The King of Benin had similar responsibilities to the English King:

1. He had extensive political powers
2. He made all the laws
3. All the taxes were paid to him

4. People needed permission from him to build houses on the land
5. The Benin king controlled all trade and commerce in his kingdom.

Only the first born son of kings could inherit their father's thrones and titles in both systems.

Whilst some of the English kings thought themselves ordained to rule by god, the Benin Kings were considered divine by their subjects.

Whilst the Benin kings built protective walls and earthen moats around their kingdom to protect their land against foreign attacks and invasion, English Kings and nobilities built protective moats of mostly water around their individual castles.

## Palace People

Both the English and the Benin had lots of people who worked in the palace, these included:

Chiefs or Lords
Palace officials
Family members,
Royal attendants
Musicians
Story teller
Servants
Cooks
Maids
Steward
Pages
Cleaners or Scullers

Both Kingdoms commissioned specialists to do certain works:
Blacksmiths
Carpenters
Builders
Wood carvers and Stonemasons

Some differences between both kingdoms these were:
The Kings of England married one wife whilst Kings of Benin married several wives. In the British system, the king had several mistresses whom the queens had to accommodate.

The Kings of England had stone masons whilst kings of Benin had blacksmiths, wood carvers and pottery workers. Can you think of a reason for this difference?

The kings of England were constantly leading wars against claimants to their thrones; whereas, the Benin Kingdom had a clear line of succession understood by all. Life was thus more peaceful for the Kingdom of Benin kings.

The kings of England led their barons and Lords in wars whilst the King of Benin never did any fighting, his specialist and well trained soldiers did all the fighting.

The king of Benin never left his palace, whilst the King of England travelled throughout his land visiting his lords and ladies in their castles. They held great feasts for him during his visits.

The kings of England commissioned tapestries to record events, Kings of Benin commissioned his blacksmiths, word carvers and terracotta workers to do so.

The English Monks wrote things down on paper, the Benin elders used oral stories, woodwork and terracotta to record their history.

## Comparing the pecking order in both kingdoms

The order of hierarchy for both systems was:

| Medieval England | Medieval Benin |
|---|---|
| English **King** ruled all the country. | **King** of Benin ruled all the country. |
| **Barons**<br><br>- Swore allegiance to the king<br>- Held vast areas of land<br>- Controlled the knights | **Titled Chiefs**<br><br>- Uzama Chiefs installed new kings, defenders of Benin customs<br>- Palace Chiefs looked after the palace<br>- Town Chiefs ran the towns |
| **Knights** defended the country when needed. | **Soldiers** defended the country against aggressors.<br><br>They were constantly asked to help protect neighbouring countries against aggressors. |
| **Freemen**<br><br>Owed no land and paid taxes to the Barons. | **Ordinary citizens**<br><br>Owed no land and paid taxes to the King. |
| **Serfs** worked for the land they lived on and had no rights. | **Slaves** worked for their keep and had no rights. |
| Serfs were tied to the land they worked on as peasants and could not move around without their Lord's permission. | Slaves worked in the households they owed a debt. They could visit their families by arrangement. |

| Serfs died without rights throughout their life time. | Slaves could work out their term and gain rights as other citizens. |
|---|---|
| Serfs were never allowed to mix with the gentry. | A slave could marry into the master's household. |
| A serf remained a serf for life. | The fortunes of a slave could change at any time. Some slaves became very rich. |

### Activity 2

Imagine that whilst you were still on your journey to the medieval kingdoms, one of the English kings has just received news that his cousin is planning a revolt to over throw him. Write a breaking news story to report the standoff between them. You could use an imaginary king or research one of the medieval Kings.

### Activity 3

Imagine that whilst you were in the kingdom of Benin, the soldiers returned from a war victorious. Draw a bronze plaque that the king would have commissioned to record this victory. Who will show on the bronze plaque?

### Activity 4

Historical enquiry: now imagine that you have returned home from your journey, write letters to both king of England and King of Benin, telling them about an interesting fact or two you learnt about their kingdoms.

### Activity 5

Now visit the Kingdom of Benin website:
kingdomofbenin.weebly.com

Complete some of the activities. Write a review of your historical enquiry into the Kingdom of Benin:

1. WWW – What worked well?
2. EBI – What could have been even better? (Even Better if).

Share your review and reflection with your class.

## Activities on the whole book

### History

- Write some facts about the kingdom of Benin

### Myths

- Read the Bini creation story; draw a cartoon strip of key events in the story.

Rewrite this story in your own words.

### The Oba or king

The king owned all the land and controlled all trade within the kingdom.

- What are the advantages and disadvantages of this system?
- Only the king can decide on capital punishment. Imagine that you are a lawyer representing a person accused of shooting a hunter dead in the forest. Write a defence speech you will present to the Oba to spare your client's life. All murders are punishable by the death penalty in Bini.

### A Chief's house

- Use a shoe box to made model of a Chief's house using the plan.

### Benin Week
The Benin people counted their weeks in four days.

- Imagine you travelled back in time to visit the kingdom. Write a daily plan of activities you would like to take part in on your visit for the week.
- Imagine that during your visit, you stayed at the palace. Write a description of the palace. Use the Dutch Dapper 1668 description of the palace to help you.
- Imagine that one of the things you did was forest exploration with some local people or a person. Write an adventure story of your time in the forest.

### Trade
The Bini people traded with a wide range of people from across the world.

- Collect 6 food labels from your kitchen and find out which country each food came from.
- Get a blank map of the word and use arrows to show each food's journey to your country. E.g. for a banana imported from Spain, draw an arrow from Spain to Britain.
- Research and list food items that are imported from different continents of the world. Draw each food item on the continent it comes from on your world map.
- Find out which food items cannot be imported into the country from other countries.

### Food
The Bini people ate different food from the rainforest and rivers.

- List 10 food items that are products of the rainforest.
- Compare the Benin diet with yours. What are the same and what are the differences.

## Celebration time

Benin people celebrated lots of festivals. During this time, each household would cook cauldrons of food and have an open door policy so that visitors throughout the day could have enough food to eat. During the festival period, all households were expected to have enough and not run out of drinks or food.

- Write a list of celebration food they cooked.
- Plan a party menu for your class end of year party.
- Try out one of the Edo recipes and write a review of the food.

## Gods' hierarchy

The Benin people believed in many gods who intervened in their daily lives. Each god had an area of responsibility.

- Write a description of each of the Benin gods.
- Write out the gods names on card and arrange them in order of importance.
- Write out the names of the gods on cards. Write out the godly responsibilities and match god to responsibility.

## Art

Benin kings used different art forms to record significant events in their history. These included bronze plaques, wood carvings and terracotta sculptors.

- Visit a museum or use internet photographs to study a Benin bronze plaque.
- Make a drawing of the plaque.
- Choose a Benin bronze plaque showing a celebration scene and any famous painting about an event of the past. Compare both of them, which captures the event more vividly? Which

method do you prefer and why? What are the advantages and disadvantages of each method of recording events in history?

### Say Cheese

- Design a plaque which will show important event in your schools' sports day. This could be to do with awards giving or someone winning a race etc. Who will you include in your plaque to really show importance of their contribution to the sports day?

### Terracotta sculptors

- Use clay to make figures head figures of your classmates or of yourself.

### Drama and role play

The Binis did not go to the theatre to see plays and shows, instead they were entertained by masquerades shows which showed scenes of interaction between the spirit world and and the tangible world. This they called 'spirits coming to the world to punish or reward people.'

- Write mythical story about a child who would not listen to his parents and is eventually taken away by spirits.
- Design a masquerade masks for a class play production of your mythical story above or another mythical story. Remember that you need a mask for each character in your story. You also need to plan dance moves to show character actions e.g. of fury and fear.
- Present this play to your whole school assembly.
- Design posters to invite parents to your masquerade show above.

## **Music**

The Binis take every opportunity to sing and dance. This is shown in their bronze plaques and their present day practices.

- Select musical instruments to make a musical composition to represent character feelings and actions in your play above
- In groups, make a musical composition to represent weather conditions for the Benin seasons of Rainy and dry seasons.
- Present your composition to the rest of the class or at school assembly.

## **It's war**

Benin soldiers were well trained and very skilled. They had advanced knowledge of science so that they could use armlets which they wore during wartimes to remain invisible to their enemies. This superior knowledge and skill made them feared by all others along the West African coast (confirmed by the British Punitive Expedition experience: Bacon, 1897, p57).

- Research Benin soldiers and write some key facts about them.
- In role as a Benin soldier make a dairy entry of a day in a war you took part in.
- In role as a spectator in a welcoming home ceremony, make a dairy entry of the celebration for the victorious Benin soldiers.
- In role as a Benin elder, write a welcome home speech for the soldiers.
- Write a public notice from the palace informing the public about this upcoming event.

## Putting down roots

Read this Wikipedia entry:

*Igueben was founded around 1516, during the reign of the Benin monarch, Oba Esigie (1504–1550), who was one of the warrior kings of the great kingdom.*

*War had broken out between the Kingdom of Benin and the Attah of the Igala Kingdom based at Idah, a town on the banks of the Niger River. Oba Esigie sent warriors in pursuit of men from Idah who had invaded Benin City. The Igala kingdom subsequently had to pay a yearly tribute to the Oba for this transgression.*

- Rewrite this information in your own words. What title will you use?

## Childhood and Education

Children in the kingdom of Benin did not go to school as we know it. Instead girls were taught at home by their mothers on good housing keeping and boys learnt their fathers' trades.

- Think about your own education. List the differences between the way you are educated and the way the Benin children were educated. List any similarities between both systems
- Read the training of Odigie the palace apprentice; write a time table of his day.

## Fashion

Benin people liked to adorn themselves. The bronzes plaques show that the royalty wore lots of coral beads. Coral beads in modern times have become an essential fashion accessory for the rich across West Africa.

- Design a traditional African lady's costume with coral beads.
- Design an accompanying man's costume.
- Use the internet to research African fashion, make drawings of their jewellery.

- Compare Nigerian traditional costume to British traditional costume. What are the same for men and women? What are different? Which do you prefer and why?

## **Hall of fame**

The Kingdom of Benin kings achieved different feats during their reign.

- Research a famous Benin king and write a simple facts file about him.

## **Review of Kingdom of Benin historical enquiry**

What did you learn from this unit?

What did you find interesting?

Did anything surprise you? What and Why?

Did you find any part of the unit challenging? Which and why??

What new information did you learn about Black and African History?

What are your views on Black and African history now?

What project will you undertake during next year's Black History Month?

What further studies are you going to carry out after completing this unit?

Summarise this project in one word.

Website: www.kingofbenin.weebly.com

Printed in Great Britain
by Amazon.co.uk, Ltd.,
Marston Gate.